Lyrica's Journey OF Ascension

ALSO BY GAYLE BARKLEY LEE AND
LYRICA MIA MARQUEZ

AWETIZM: A HIDDEN KEY TO OUR
SPIRITUAL MAGNIFICENCE

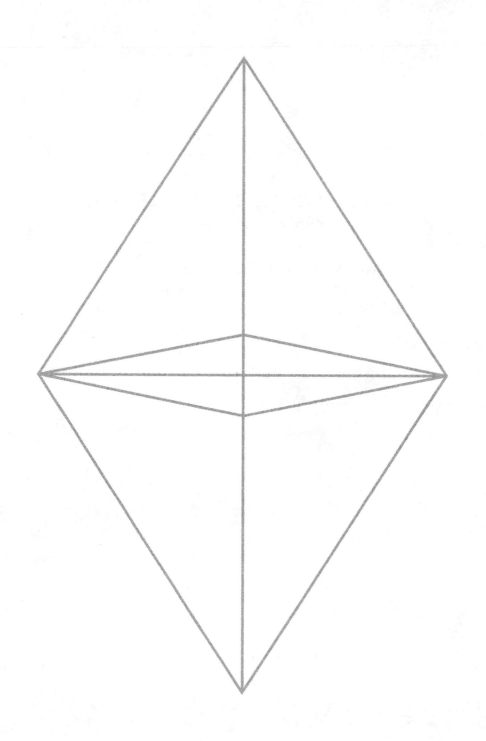

Lyrica's Journey OF Ascension

A NONVERBAL AUTISTIC FINDS HER
POWER, PEACE, AND PURPOSE

BY LYRICA MARQUEZ & GAYLE LEE

Mialee LLC
Sedona, Arizona

Mialee LLC
Sedona, Arizona
Copyright © 2021 by Gayle Lee & Lyrica Marquez. All rights reserved.
Library of Congress Control Number: 2021910951
Paperback ISBN: 978-1-7365621-0-9
eBook ISBN: 978-1-7365621-1-6

Book cover design by Wendy Allison
Interior design by Christina Thiele and Wendy Allison
Editorial production by kn literary
www.lyricaandgayle.com
Printed in the United States of America

This book is dedicated to all the nonverbal autistics (NVAs) who are here to support humanity's Ascension process.

They chose to lightly incarnate on earth to retain their connection to Source and their own higher frequency. They are here to deliver their gift of light into humanity's heart and into the politics of separation that rule the planet right now.

Think about how much they must love us to choose to come into a world that is not a vibrational match, without a voice, in a body that functions poorly! Most struggle to simply be here. Sadly, many don't even know why they are here and the important role that they are playing.

Lyrica demonstrates her extraordinary love for us through her journey of Ascension.

contents

ACT I:
THE DESCENT

contents

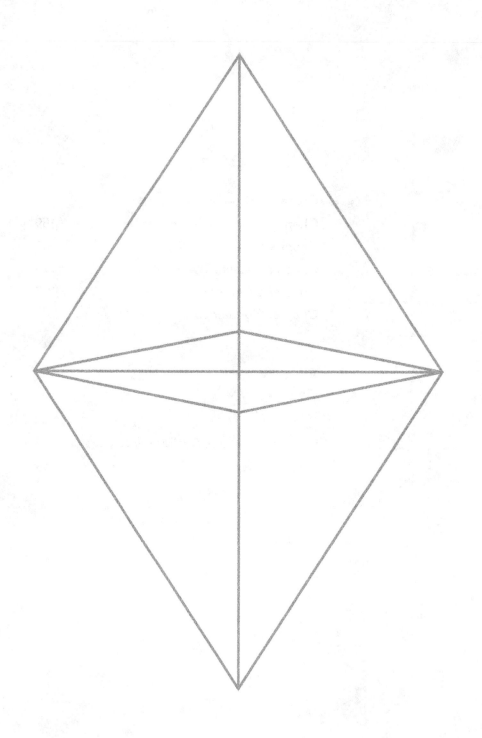

Introduction

If you are a person who believes that you are here to make a difference, and passionately want to do just that, then our story is your story!

The abilities and training that we all need to fulfill this vision are within us, but they remain under lock and key in the deepest recesses of our being. There is only one way to unearth that which is hidden: crack the codes, win the prize, and emerge victorious. The path of Ascension is that doorway, that road map, that human drama, that starlit path. It is the epic journey toward *becoming fully human*. It is the heartbeat that gives us life. It is the soul call that will persist until it is heard. It is the soul mandate that is forever nudging us into action.

No matter where we are, we are here to do this work, regardless of whatever else we *think* we may be here to do! Nothing is more important. Nothing less will satisfy the soul. Nothing else will prepare us and place us in the position to truly make a difference in this world. There are no shortcuts, no free passes, no substitutes.

Lyrica tells us that this journey is the only path that truly matters! Our souls have only one objective in this current incarnation, and that is to step solidly into our own hero's journey. Anything short of that is a waste of time and energy and will only serve to keep us trapped in endless cycles of suffering. Hallelujah for this suffering! Its ever-increasing pain is our wake-up call, our call to arms. Only when the pain gets unbearable will we be brave enough to pick up our walking sticks and begin the journey to the land where all heroes must dare to tread.

The journey to Ascension begins with a choice, one that is made by our tiny selves, often hopeless, broken, and lost, or perhaps "puffed up" and overconfident. Once begun, how does it unfold?

Be advised that this journey will ask of us more than we ever believed we could possibly endure and survive. It is the highest possible challenge, because the soul goal for each one of us who answers the call is to enter into Oneness, the realm of total transformation, and emerge as a whole and vibrant being—and then to bring our gift of Self back into the community, back home. That's when the ordinary of "all that we see, know, and experience" becomes the extraordinary of "The All That Is!" That's when we finally know that we have arrived into our truth. We are now transformed travelers. We are what the world is waiting for. We are the *new consciousness pioneers.*

As new consciousness pioneers, we are the reformers and revolutionaries who hold the power, presence, and promise to change the course of history forever. New consciousness can literally change physicality in a moment, in a positive way, and thereby create new solutions and outcomes to some of humanity's most pressing challenges. The keys to a better world rest in our hands! The change that this world desperately needs begins within each one of us.

This book is written to impart an active transmission directly into the heart and soul of all new consciousness pioneers. It is a call to action! It is a call to community. It is a call to play our part in humanity's global Ascension process, which is already well underway. It is also a call to let go of the slippery slope of pursuing success, material possessions, and self-gratification in favor of seeking the more elusive soul-satisfying, heart-filled treasures of the spirit.

For this is our highest quest as humans. It is the only one that can carry us into uncharted territories, where our own happiness, joy, creativity, and love are freely flowing, waiting for us to arrive! Here is where we all can thrive!

This is our land of plenty, where there is no more us and them, right and wrong, women and men, leaders and followers. Here, there are no more positive or negative experiences. Instead, all experiences simply become stepping stones to help us reach higher pinnacles in Oneness. From there, we can begin to harness our own Superpowers to work in concert with the entire Universe. Some may even reach levels of self-mastery and become able to command the Universe to manifest higher reality outcomes for all.

The greatest gift that we can impart to the children of planet earth is to become a conscious, creative, manifesting being, someone who is impassioned to make the world a better place, where all are equal and all can thrive. Only then can we move closer into becoming one world, one humanity, no longer separated by national origin, social or economic class, racial differences, ethnic identity, religious affiliation, educational level, or any other divisions we have placed among ourselves.

That's the only way to solve the larger problems of hunger, poverty, discrimination, violence, war, and greed. These worldwide disparities and grave inequalities *cannot be shifted* from within the same mind-heart state that created them. Creating a new order from within a higher dimensional space is the agenda of the new consciousness pioneers.

Join Lyrica and me, two unlikely heroines, on a wild and raw soul ride into experiences guaranteed to stun, delight, and inspire you in your own hero's journey, whether you are just starting out at this moment, venturing forth, totally lost, or if you are already a seasoned traveler. Our story reveals that even someone who is considered to have arrived into this life with more limitations than most, can, in the end, become victorious. Lyrica clearly demonstrates that all that we *are*, and all that we *have*, is all that we *need* to fulfill our human imperative to become fully realized as a unique soul in union with the whole of humanity and the Greater Universe, the All That Is.

As you read our story, we hope that you will carry it with you in your heart. We passionately implore you to believe in yourself and know that you are perfectly formed and informed for your mission, regardless of how your present situation may feel or look. We have faith that against all odds, you will persevere to accomplish that which is totally amazing and totally, authentically you.

One thing to point out is that we use different fonts depending on who is speaking.

Lyrica's direct words are set in this font. When you see this typeface, you'll know you're reading a section by Lyrica. (This font is called New June.)

When Gayle is speaking, she does so in this font. In other words, the sections by Gayle are set in this typeface. (This font is called Transat Text.)

As we set forth, we would like to get you familiar with a few terms we use often. These words will serve as a map for your journey throughout this book.

Ascension

We once thought of Ascension as a privileged experience that could be attained by saints after death or haloed mystics on mountaintops. But this is not the case. In today's world, Ascension belongs to all of us. It is the journey of becoming fully unified in Oneness, the All That Is, the Universe, the Creator, Source, God. It is the quest for self-realization. It is you and I living our truth by fulfilling our purpose as divine beings having a human experience.

We Ascend by unifying our physical and nonphysical natures and by balancing and unifying our Feminine and Masculine essences. Although the ultimate quest is to "arrive," every step along the way is a gift of soul evolution.

The division between the physical and nonphysical aspects of ourselves is often cited as the disconnect between the body and the soul/spirit. It can also be thought of as the disconnect between the ego-driven self and the higher self, our human and Cosmic essence, or simply our humanity and our divinity.

Believing that our bodies represent the totality of ourselves is a great tragedy of the human experience. This separation is the source of much societal malaise. A body as a stand-alone vehicle will never give us what we truly need or want. Without unification with the spirit/soul, humanity is doomed to follow its cultural programming to live life for self-gratification in a frenetic race against time and aging.

This strategy pushes away (for a while) the shadow of emptiness that lives within this lifestyle. Yet, at some point, the body and its legs can no longer move fast enough to avoid the spirit's/soul's ever-encroaching wake-up call. A life crisis often becomes the catalyst that shuts down the race and allows the unification process between the body and spirit/soul to begin.

On the other hand, those who identify exclusively with our spiritual nature also miss the mark. They believe that Ascension is attained when one has a profound spiritual awakening and reaches a high-frequency state of being, but that's only half true. Ascension can only be experienced by grounding a state of enlightenment in a physical body.

Part of that process involves connecting with both the Feminine and the Masculine. As a society, we have become separated from our true Feminine nature, yet deep within the pain of not knowing Her lives an equally powerful pull to seek, find, and unify that which has been lost or forgotten. For She is the one who knows our truth. She is the voice of our intuition. She is the heart-holder of love without fear and of freedom without boundaries. She is the energy that empowers us as creator beings, and the essence that nurtures all life.

Side by side with the Feminine stands Her complement, the Masculine. If the Feminine is the intuitive knower and flow-er of our truth, it is the Masculine who then becomes the protector, the actor, and the manifester of that truth in the world. It is the oscillation between the two, united as one, that brings to "light" highly charged divine manifestations.

In today's world, those in power who strive to harm, force, control, program, manipulate, even enslave, represent the leadership of an unbalanced male archetype. Reinstalling the presence of the Feminine into our world is the only way to bring this male archetype into balance. Each one of us can do our part by striving to unify our own Feminine and Masculine essences.

It is when we bring all these together—the body, the spirit/soul, the Feminine, and the Masculine—that we experience Ascension.

Embodiment and Gridding

Arriving here as a lightly incarnated being, I retained a powerful connection to my spirit/soul. The main focus of my journey of Ascension was to embody this vast essence of me. Mom, like most earth beings, arrived here disconnected from her spiritual nature. Reconnecting to that awareness became the major goal of her path of Ascension.

Regardless of where one begins, the process of embodiment is required. It is a universal soul-assignment of humanity's call to Ascend. Embodying our higher consciousness is key to the leadership that our planet desperately needs now.

Working with the earth's grid is another way of assisting humanity's Ascension process. Nonverbal autistics (NVAs) and lightworkers we call "gridders" know how to release energetic trauma from the grid's patterning and anchor in a higher light frequency. These grid advancements help stabilize our Ascension process, and as we Ascend, we help to light up the grid.

Oneness

The primal essence of Oneness is the "loss of separation." Three easy sounding words that seem to disappear as quickly as they are said or thought. Oneness seems so simple. Yet landing it is the most colossal undertaking of a superhero, demanding a level of prowess that defies all boundaries of the human condition.

We are bred to believe in edges beyond which there is no possibility of escape or passage. How strange that the outer edges of our mind dictate our reality! Our mind's ability to see and believe in that which cannot be seen or known through its linear capabilities of perception is a direct measure of how expanded we can become. What a conundrum! If this mind condition is our navigational compass and our trusted pathfinder, are we therefore locked into forever following the roads printed on the map? Or do we at some point dare to get off the trail and forge our way through jungles and swamps, facing encounters in the dark that freeze our steps, strangle our voice, and rapid-fire our hearts to pound voraciously against the walls of our chest, as if to scare away the demons that threaten our very survival?

Yes. This adventure off the path is what is required for us to lose our identity as separate beings having a separated experience in a separated life within a separated world. No wonder our mind shrinks away from and quickly discards the very idea of "loss of separation!"

Yet there is a deeper reason for its avoidance. Loss of separation means the death of the ego, and the ego is the imposter who rules and commands in our absence. It is the lord of our mind's field, or its own minefield playground that keeps us reacting to explosions of fear that trigger us into flight, freeze, or fight. The games that it plays to keep us off-balance are its very clever way of maintaining its supremacy.

In this scenario, we lose sight of our universal connectedness, our divinity, of life's abundance and joy—in essence, our true nature. Our voice forgets to sing, our feet forget to dance, our hands forget to create, and our eyes no longer see the beauty all around us.

We trudge through each day, head bowed and heart heavy, living in a state of mere survival. We lose access to our life's purpose, our gifts, and our soul's power to create and manifest. Even more devastating, we lose our connection to Oneness, where all the wisdom, gifts, love, and power of the entire Universe are waiting to be bestowed upon us.

But if we can step past the ego and past the mind's fears, we can freely shed our forbidden tears, withheld to not appear weak. We can heal our brokenness and begin to remember our truth. This is not an easy reach, for it requires us to move into a place of Oneness with Source, above our normal experience of separation and duality. It is possible, however, if we consciously dedicate ourselves to the practice and development of new skills.

The amazing thing is that even if we never reach Ascension, just the pursuit alone can change our inner and outer worlds, filled with both pearls and perils. We will face new challenges, and when we stumble into them, they may strike a note of terror within us, almost like stepping on a rattlesnake coiled in our path. But this rattlesnake is nothing more than a representation of our inner demons, which are only scary because we aren't used to seeing them. Once they are fully seen in the light of their truth, they shapeshift into magical parts of us, forgotten but never fully lost. These gifts then become our seasoned staff as we faithfully journey on.

Beloveds, it is time to once again reclaim our truth as gentle giants who walk upon the earth, sovereign and free, blissfully being who we truly are, bonding in love to one another, finding our purpose, and contributing to humanity and the planet in our own unique and perfect way. This is living dimensionally, unbounded by time, space, or any other perceived constraints. This is living in ease and grace. This is the true path forward! This is Oneness in action.

How can we know Oneness or the state of "no more

separation"? There is only one way "in." It is through *direct experience* of being in a dimensional zone above the 3D realm. Here we lose awareness of the "I of me" that disappears into the totality of the All That Is. Here we experience Universal Essence, God-Essence. Here we are only light and love. Here we have transcended into pure bliss!

This holy experience was my norm for most of my early life, something that I now know as an out-of-body experience. Yet since I have become more embodied, the quality and possibilities within my experience of Oneness have changed. Being unified with Source has now awakened a new awareness in me that I, too, am a creator. This more embodied experience of Oneness is my path of empowerment to know and express my truth and purpose as a physical being in a physical world.

Superpowers

Superpowers are the often latent or lost abilities that all humans have. These abilities enable us to access, experience, and even command higher dimensional worlds and energy. They are the powers wielded by the alchemist, the magician, the wizard. Perhaps most familiar are our multidimensional gifts, like clairaudience, the ability to "hear"; clairvoyance, the ability to "see"; and clairsentience, the ability to "feel" beyond the physical and into nonphysical reality.

As someone just beginning to explore Superpowers, I will be speaking not as an expert but as one who is learning and loving what's possible here! Everything moves from energy into form, and that means that any object that exists here in our 3D world, is malleable. In the higher dimensions, energy can be shifted to influence, even change physical reality. This is how an energy healer creates miraculous outcomes, like reducing or eradicating a cancerous tumor in the body.

When we rise above the 3D physical plane and are present in 5D is when we gain access to our own Superpowers and become co-creators and change agents, supported by all the powers of the Universe. From the 5D state, we can ladder up into even higher states of consciousness and use our highly focused mind, powerful will, and Superpowers to command the manifestation of energy to benefit ourselves, others, and the planet. The keys belong to each of us. We just have to unlock the door and enter.

The crossover

between 3D to 5D is the greatest step that any human can take. It has little to do with the outer world. It is a total recalibration of our inner world. It is a higher vibration of the heart that informs and directs every thought and action of our body and being. It is like living in a wonderland where there are no more opposites, just harmony and love.

Once I stabilized my crossover into 5D and above, I developed new Superpowers, like bilocating, or being in two places at the same time. I first acquired this ability, or light technology, as a coded transmission. The more connected I became to my physical body and its higher dimensional access, the more advanced and focused my Superpowers became. All these upgrades came as gifts to support my purpose—and the same will be true for you.

Join the journey!

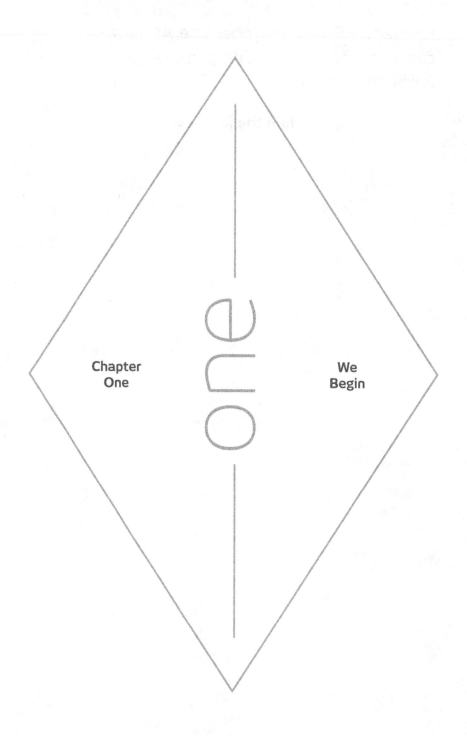

Chapter
One

one

We
Begin

I wonder how many people have ever truly considered what it might be like to be here without a speaking voice for forty-five years? Or how it might feel to be a person who is labeled as severely autistic?

My early years were bleak and dark. I was trapped in a body that I didn't even know was mine. In fact, there wasn't any **me** that I remember. My only awareness was the constant input of pain I received from sounds, touch, and simply being here, existing. I felt nothing but a desperate desire to stop the pain.

As I became more aware of my human form, I began to understand my situation. I could not do anything for myself and required total care. I had to endure endless hours of physical therapy to teach my body to sit, stand, walk, and try to do other things that humans can do. I did eventually develop mobility, but the rest of the human programming did not imprint. Instead, what imprinted was a belief that I was a human failure.

The people around me meant to be kind, but I experienced them as agents of perpetual pain. I had no control. I could not even scream to let my pain out. I began to feel this pervasive pain as the truth of what I was. I **was** pain! I was trapped forever and there could be no escape.

This feeling only intensified when I started public school. My anger erupted, often in violent tantrums, and then my explosive nature moved into severe seizure episodes, seizure falls, and trips to the ER. I desperately wanted to die, yet I did not know how to kill myself.

But then, at age eight, everything changed. My world of silence was shattered. I intuitively developed a unique process to communicate with my mom through typing. Over time, this communication breakthrough evolved into a mutual ability to share thoughts telepathically. As I found my voice, I found myself! For the first time ever, I was feeling more in control. I now had a tool to find the real me.

Telling this story with my mom, Gayle, feels like a piece of my life's completion, and I know that for her, too, it is equally powerful.

So, who am I really? My nonspeaking autistic nature no longer describes who I am, not by a long shot! Yet thanks to my lightly incarnated state as an NVA, I have been able to become so much more than most people could ever imagine. How could that be? What's the riddle here? It has taken me decades to decode this mystery!

What is our soul's truth and purpose? What is Oneness? What is Ascension? Can souls consciously choose and create their own Ascension process? If so, how might that happen? In this book, we answer these questions and invite you to find your own path to greater consciousness and fulfillment of your expressed purpose!

Lyrica is unique, but she is also just like all of us, for the truth is that, regardless of our starting point in life, we are all here to make a difference in the world, and we can! As her mother, I want to walk you through her early life from my perspective, so that you can get a sense of just how much she has had to overcome.

As a Communication Innovator and Education Rights Advocate for the Disabled

Months before Lyrica's third birthday, the medical/educational experts had labeled her future as dismal, propelling us into action. At Philadelphia's Institutes for the Achievement of Human Potential, we were given a home-based therapy program that included teaching Lyrica to sight-read word cards. The three-inch-tall bright red letters that I artfully printed on glossy white twenty-four-inch long poster boards were the only stimuli that seemed to enter into her world. We watched her eyes move to a requested word card, and we could tell that her brain was learning to discriminate one word from another. In a body totally shut down and unresponsive to anything and everything around her, she was demonstrating that she could "read"!

Our home morphed into a massive library of word cards. Lyrica was presented with one hundred new word cards every week! Later, we began to use these cards as a way to give Lyrica choices in her day. I could ask her what she wanted to eat for breakfast and then present her with two cards like "eggs" or "oatmeal." Her eyes always rapidly landed on her preferred choice.

That's when a bright idea came to me. If she could "read," could she perhaps type a word? When Lyrica was eight years old, I brought her to my computer and invited her to talk to me. She picked up my middle finger on my right hand and started hitting keys. At first it all seemed like gibberish, yet soon I started to pick up letter combinations that suggested a word or two. Then I saw the magic sentence pop out that would change our lives forever. *iamnotretardediamintelligent*—I am not retarded, I am intelligent!

The immensity of that moment opened up a whole new life and world for us. Over time, Lyrica adjusted the process so that she was using her finger to type, and I was providing light support to stabilize her arm. For years, I had desperately longed to find a way into her world, and we had finally arrived at a meeting point. As new words emerged, I became privy to what the medical/educational "experts" could not see—the extraordinary being that was hiding inside this tiny body, waiting to be discovered. It was my heart that needed to open to "see" Lyrica's true nature, her "genius" within!

When Lyrica was fifteen, we happened by chance to see an episode of *20/20* that showed three nonverbal autistics typing just like Lyrica. We were stunned! We had no idea that anyone else on the planet was communicating in this way. The show introduced us to the work of Rosemary Crossley and Dr. Douglas Biklen. We learned that in 1977, a teacher named Rosemary Crossley was working with patients at a hospital in Australia and discovered a typing methodology to assist those who could not speak; she helped them successfully communicate by typing. Her process became known as Facilitated Typing/Facilitated Communication, or FC. In 1989, Dr. Doug Biklen of Syracuse University's School of Education, visited Rosemary Crossley to learn more about FC and the outcomes that she was reporting. Amazed by what he witnessed, he began teaching FC back in the United States, focusing primarily on assisting autistics who were nonverbal.

That episode of *20/20* aired just as we were headed into due process with the Nashville school system, requesting that Lyrica be given access to an academic education that would utilize her typing ability. Due process is a last-resort legal proceeding—in essence, it is suing the school system. It is an expensive and drawn out process, and families who turn to it have exhausted all collaborative efforts without securing the services that they believe their child deserves as his or her educational right, guaranteed by federal law.

Dr. Biklen reviewed a video of Lyrica typing and validated it as FC. Now we had a name for this process and documentation from a university that other NVAs were successfully communicating in this same way.

I learned from Dr. Biklen that a nonverbal autistic's success with FC was related to the neurological patterning of the autistic brain. The purpose of this typing support was to minimize praxis and perseveration, movements often prevalent in autistics that compromise their ability to type. In his book *Communication Unbound*, Dr. Biklen tells the story of how Lyrica independently developed this method of communication, validating its efficacy as a way to give voice to those living in silence.

This unique typing process was downloaded to me as part of my divine mission here. I needed to have a voice to begin to shape my destiny as a writer and a teacher. Once I understood the partnering role that I needed, I had to get Mom to do her part. I sent her a telepathic message: "Take me to your computer." She had no clue that her bright idea came in as a telepathic message from me! We quickly moved our typing talks from Mom's computer to an on-the-go letter board that I designed at a neighborhood sign company. I would type and Mom would record my words in a notebook.

These words inspired the writing of our first book, published in June 2011. My next inspiration to write popped in after seeing *Touch*, about Jake, a nonverbal autistic character. I wanted the whole world to see his true-to-life gift! Jake was able to "see" things energetically as patterns, before they happened, and his dad had a tuned-in ability to "read" Jake's distress signals. Lives were saved and major disasters prevented. Jake was now a silent hero on mainstream TV!

I was so charged up that I began to write a weekly blog to inspire readers to watch the latest episode of *Touch*. People responded to each blog post, loving my words and loving me. Next, I began to highlight new understandings that were waking up in me, truths about my purpose and the larger soul-group purpose of NVAs. One topic I often repeated was that we had come to earth to share our high-frequency light with others. Many lightworkers joined in the conversation. They knew that most people around us were not yet energetically organized to receive our gift of light. These lightworkers were living in a higher frequency zone than those in the mainstream. They could see our gifts and knew our challenges well. Their partnership support was a beautiful heart-gift that inspired me to keep writing. I shared many other soul-talk blogs about humanity's evolution, its future, and the light. Between February 2012 and April 2013, I wrote fifty blog posts. I gathered quite a large following and received the nickname the Autistic Mystic.

Mom has already explained how written words as language became very familiar to me on the big white cards with the bright red letters! Yet to fully communicate, I needed access to many new words that I did not yet know. Once again, what I needed, when I needed it, came through to me via a download. If I needed to spell a certain word, the letters just popped into my knowing. I quickly learned to trust in this ability. It was a soul operation.

In our first book, Lyrica described this process as a "divine unfolding." She wrote this message to me not long after she developed the ability to communicate: "I get God's love in writing. On words, He tips long top sounds my way. I get new big words from Him. I great writer in hearing God talking to my fingers typing words. Go to long typings to get God's presence. Hill on top of finger emotes language I not have. I get started lonely until I get my beautiful God gully running inside me. Happens as gift from God. Hits my fingers like putty in His hands. I hear great long ribbons of thinking waiting for typing. Typing get ribbons trilling."

Lyrica updates us on how she now views this process.

Today I would describe this flow more as my state of alignment in Oneness, Source, the Universe, the Divine, the All That Is that gifts me whatever I need, when I need it, to support my truth and purpose.

As early pioneers of this communication breakthrough, our due process case was the first in the nation that featured the use of FC. We won that case because the PhD researcher assigned to evaluate

Lyrica's process of communication documented that Lyrica's finger, in rare moments, hit a correct letter on the keyboard without any physical assistance from me.

Winning this due process case opened up Lyrica's access to academic opportunities and eventually led to her inclusion in mainstream classrooms. Yet the road was long and hard. The next victory to be won was securing Lyrica's right to a full-time facilitator. This not-so-simple feat required moving the entire Nashville educational system into a new paradigm! Lyrica was the first NVA to ever attend a mainstream classroom in the history of her high school. No one knew what to expect, including Lyrica! At times, she had to leave class early due to her noises or not being able to stay in her seat. Yet she persevered. With the aid of her facilitator, she completed homework and in-class assignments, took tests, and even did several classroom presentations using her Link communication device that had a voice synthesizer and a small paper printout, about the size of a grocery receipt.

She had several high school peers who served as "buddies" in her nonacademic classes, like physical education. In this way, she was fully included and initiated into the teenage high school scene. Supported by her facilitator, she was often present at after-hours high school events such as dances, pep rallies, and football games. As Lyrica and her facilitator crossed the stage at graduation to receive Lyrica's special education diploma, the cheers from the entire student body were the loudest of the night. She had touched their hearts.

Her gains and successes in mainstream classrooms left behind a rich legacy, one that will continue to benefit others. Even if those who followed her still remained cloistered in special education classes, educators and students alike had seen how someone who presented as severely "disabled" was in truth surprisingly capable and had much to offer.

Being me has not been easy! Being poorly regarded by others who only see the outside of me has broken my heart so many times. This was a chance to change the way that others saw me. Yet I had no idea how hard this new "grow-up assignment" would be! It wasn't the work that was so challenging, because whatever I could do was accepted by all. It was learning how to be calm in the midst of so much classroom stimulation and intense teenage energy.

That's when I began to realize how teenagers, too, are trying to fit in and be accepted for who they are. I loved watching the ones who dared to be different with their crazy clothes, funky haircuts, and rainbow-colored hair! By understanding and accepting them for who they really were, I was also learning how to better understand and accept myself for who I really am!

As an IQ Paradigm Buster

In my school years, my family and I were introduced to something called evaluations. Here, all that I could not do was highly noted as a marker of me. I particularly remember the number nineteen. Why? It was an IQ score stamped into all my evaluations, and it followed me throughout my entire school career. Mom tells me that a nineteen

IQ score is below the twenty to twenty-five IQ range used to diagnose profound mental retardation.

The school's standardized IQ test offered me no way to demonstrate the unique gifts and abilities deeply embedded in my soul to fulfill my life's purpose. Instead, it merely recorded how far away I was from "the norm," or normal patterns of development. At the time that I was tested, I had no voice to speak and could not command my body to follow instructions or make requested selections.

So I ask, was the failure mine or that of a system that was rigidly locked into "normal" as its only way to measure one's abilities and value to society?

At age twenty-three, to qualify for adult services in Tennessee, Lyrica was required to undergo another IQ test. This time I was with her. The examiner was intrigued by Lyrica's ability to type and allowed her to use FC during the testing. A significant section of the test involved Lyrica looking at a stimulus (picture or image) and explaining what it was.

Lyrica was thrilled to participate. She quickly shared a literal translation of what she saw. Then she would often comment on what she perceived as a larger meaning or significance either for herself and her life or for the world and humanity at large. She became an animated storyteller with a captive audience!

I remember noting how surprised the examiner was when Lyrica responded to a picture of a man's face with a rather disturbed look. Lyrica said that it reminded her of the way that Salvador Dali would often exaggerate facial features in his paintings! She explained that this was the artist's way of helping us perceive and feel beyond "what's normal" or "what's expected." It's this kind of surprise factor that opens up new ways of seeing.

We were shocked when we got a letter saying that Lyrica scored above seventy in her IQ test, which meant that she was *not* "retarded"! In a follow-up meeting, the examiner shared that she was blown away by Lyrica's ability to perceive in a gestalt-like way and communicate symbolically at a level far above the norm. She saw her abilities as rare and exceptional!

At age forty-one, to validate her eligibility for new adult services, Lyrica was once again required to undergo an IQ test. The PhD examiner explained to both of us that he would be evaluating Lyrica using a nonverbal IQ test. One portion of this protocol involved pattern recognition. Lyrica was shown an intricate line drawing and then asked to find its exact match in a group of three closely related images.

This was like putting Brer Rabbit in the Briar Patch! Lyrica selected matching images in a nanosecond. The examiner commented on Lyrica's ability to select matches so quickly and accurately. Based on this nonverbal testing protocol, Lyrica received an IQ score of sixty-four.

So, what is the point here? Lyrica's IQ test results over her lifetime challenge today's prevailing belief that one's IQ is inherent and unchangeable.

I want my NVA beloveds to know that your IQ score is not a measure of your abilities or your value to society. Far from it. The higher wisdom that we hold and the masters of light that we are cannot be seen or measured in an IQ test that is focused solely on mental-plane functioning. As such, IQ tests totally miss the mark on who we are and why we are here. (However, they are often what is required for us and our families to gain access to the community services that we need and deserve.)

As a Proponent of Telepathy

Lyrica cites telepathy as her most natural and, in many ways, most beloved language of communication. However, it can only be used effectively when partnered with a person who has developed his or her own telepathic skills and abilities. It is like having someone on the other end of the telephone who knows how to listen. Lyrica's decision to engage in telepathy requires a partner with an open heart and a frequency that is harmonic with hers, and is someone who holds a very precise platform of trust. These same tenets are also what she requires for sharing messages with another via her unique typing method.

Trusting in my ability to receive downloads when needed is similar to learning to trust in telepathy as a form of higher communication. In telepathy, the unspoken words simply flow between a transmitter and a receiver. When I engage in telepathy, I silently hear words from another in my mind. Early on, I named this process "mind-talking."

My experience with this process first began with other nonverbal autistics. In my early school years, mind-talking with my NVA classmates offered me stimulation and an escape from a classroom curriculum that was boring and meaningless. We laughed at the way the school wanted us to conform. Teachers saw us as flat tires and tried to fix us. It was a different kind of tire that no one understood!

Using my telepathic abilities, I am able to hear people's thoughts and tune into their soul messages. When I do, I sometimes pick up their soul wounds, input that is not easy for my heart to receive! Yet what my heart loves most is sharing telepathic conversations with my mom. To us, telepathic communication is normal and natural and certainly very honoring to me as an equal participant without any communication barriers. It is my preferred language and that of my soul group. For us, telepathic communication holds a higher frequency and spans a wider dimensional reach than speaking or writing.

So how did Mom and I become telepathic? In our early years together, Mom's thoughts about me were influenced by the outside world. A close doctor friend strongly recommended that Mom institutionalize me. His reason was that severely retarded children grow up into severely retarded adults. He believed that our family life would be destroyed by having to managing someone like me.

Once Mom realized my intelligence, a light doorway opened up for telepathy to develop. I heard how much she wanted to know the *real* me and all that I was thinking. Each time I would type a few words, Mom held them dearly like clues into the great mystery of me. I did not have the ability to organize my thoughts into a language that was easy for her to understand. I heard her many questions popping up like popcorn as I slowly typed words-touching-words. We were both hungry to talk to each other, but my early typings were too slow to allow for a real conversation.

My mind started to answer the questions that her mind was asking. Often, she would translate my words into her own words to better understand them. Then she would ask, "Is *this* what you are saying to me?" Bingo, she got it! She was hearing me telepathically!

Mom would say what she thought she was "hearing," and I would confirm it with my typing. When we were both in Oneness, our mind-to-mind flow was fluid and word-by-word accurate. Finally, we no longer needed a typing confirmation—we both just knew!

As a Pillar of Mother-Daughter Devotion

There is a natural tension within the dynamics of most parent-child relationships, as boundaries are tested and expectations are not met. When Lyrica was fourteen, we made a life-long contract: Lyrica would be in charge of every decision in her life, and I would only hold veto powers in the areas of hygiene and safety. Not only did this arrangement reduce potential areas of conflict, it established a soul-blessing environment and partnership that has allowed both of us to flourish.

In the physical department, Mom is definitely the care provider and I am the care receiver. Yet in the spiritual department, I am the care provider and she is the care receiver. This wonderful exchange allows for equality and an appreciation of each of our contributions and gifts to one other. When the vast spiritual gifts of the NVA are merged with the physically embodied gifts of the parent, a new sense of power and purpose is born. This synthesis is a divine unfolding that empowers the choice that was made to incarnate together in this lifetime. It creates an energetic template that can empower other NVA families in developing a similar platform of creative partnership. This aligned relationship dynamic has stabilized both of us through the intensity and quickening of our process of Ascension. The truth or "divine essence" of our partnership has emerged out of our journey into Oneness. Through it, we have been able to access new levels of power to create the life that we are now living and sharing in this story of love.

As an Author and Writer

Having attended mainstream classrooms in high school, Lyrica contemplated going to college. She wanted to prove her abilities and worth to herself and others. But once she learned to tap into her own soul's wisdom stream, she realized that her truth and her life's purpose could be best found in her own independent writing and learning.

After the release of *AWEtizm* and Lyrica's later blogs, a profound number of readers reported how deeply impacted they were by Lyrica's words and messages. Many shared their own personal stories of how Lyrica's writings enhanced their spiritual development, often empowering them to address a particular life challenge in a more soul-aligned way. Through their stories, Lyrica became aware that there were codes of light embedded in her written expressions, creating transmissions that could activate a soul-awakening in her readers. Being a writer allowed her to support humanity's path of Ascension.

It is interesting for me to note how much my communication style has changed over time. Early typings were simpler and more poetic in tone. In that way, they were very endearing. Now, in my more embodied and conscious state, my voice has become more matter-strong, more conceptual and complex. This enhanced ability enables me to step strongly into my destiny as a "voice" to inspire other new consciousness pioneers.

I was thirty when Lyrica was born. In learning to care for her, as her ways defied all the child-rearing manuals and mantras, I began to develop my own lesson plans for "parenting for the soul." I was learning how to love, even when Lyrica showed no recognition or acceptance of me. I was learning to love in spite of the nonstop flow of daily demands that Lyrica's care required. This level of giving demanded even more of me after her father and I parted ways and I became a full-time single mom. I didn't know it, but my journey toward self-actualization was now in high gear.

Asperger's Syndrome

I had just finished reading an article in *The Autism Perspective* written by Taylor Cross entitled "Normal People Scare Me." I was stunned! They scared me too! His story was my story!

That's when I realized something I had buried deep: Lyrica and the other NVAs in my life were my first and only safe friends! In their presence, I felt at ease and understood. Their unconditional love and acceptance of me gave me the freedom I needed to release the programming of protection and find the real me. Together we have shared a powerful journey of awakening.

In this journey, the more I began to understand the NVA's inner world through their writings, the more I dared to acknowledge the similarities between my life and theirs. I ventured into a very reputable mental health clinic in Phoenix that specialized in working with people on the autism spectrum. At age sixty, my connection to and passion for those with autism had come full circle, as I myself received a formal diagnosis as a person with Asperger's syndrome, considered to be a mild form of autism.

Uplifted by this confirmation, I could now courageously look back at my life, finally able to own the level of sheer terror that had plagued my inner being day and night. On the surface, I had mastered masking my fears and pretending all was well. Yet the more accomplished I became in this disguise, the more I lost connection to my true self!

Simple things that the rest of the world took for granted eluded me. I could not follow the plot of a book or movie with more than one timeline or storyline occurring simultaneously, as the complexities were just too difficult for me to sort out and assimilate. I was totally perplexed by humor, like in a comic strip. I had to have someone explain to me the subtle details of each frame and their progression, when lined up side by side, that would normally and automatically register as funny for most viewers.

A much larger everyday challenge for me was having to go to work to financially support Lyrica and myself. Although I managed to hold a few meaningful jobs, my pattern was to stay in a professional setting no more than a couple of years. My workplace survival hinged on spending as many hours as possible inside my own office, far away from the break room where colleagues gathered to share friendship and casual conversation. Burying myself in work was my ideal strategy for avoiding the social complexities of the workplace.

My greatest nightmare of all would be an invitation to a party or any kind of social gathering. For starters, due to an aspect of autism known as "face blindness," I often could not recognize people I had previously met. To compensate, when meeting someone new, I would scan their face for a "standout" feature or mark that I could literally memorize and link to their name in order to later recall their identity. Sometimes it worked, but many times it did not. Not being able to remember people who obviously knew me dropped me quickly into a state of social anxiety.

The moment that I stepped into any social gathering, I was instantly overwhelmed by group dynamics that I could not sort through, and all the subtle social cues that normally inform human interactions—cues that I could not read. I felt like a stranger in a strange land. I had little interest in the topics that were being discussed, or I simply had no clue what people were talking about.

People would say things and everyone would laugh, but not me. I just didn't "get it." I got very good at nodding my head and pasting on that empty smile, the one that covered up my pain of not understanding and not belonging. I kept wondering what the heck was wrong with me. To escape, I spent as much time as I could in the bathroom or other hiding places, waiting for it to all be over.

What I now realize is that their conversations were way too fast-paced for my mind, as I process things slowly and deeply. Their exchanges quickly flat-lined in my brain, as if I were listening to a foreign language. If I tried to join in and say anything, my words always hung in the air as a rather ridiculous, out-of-sync comment. I felt shame and embarrassment. I stopped listening. I stopped trying.

I wanted to run away or simply disappear to escape the cascade of sensations that dropped me into a place of feeling so alone, so unsafe, so scrambled. If this was life, what was the point?

I now know the answer! Like Lyrica, my autism has served as a perfect backdrop for my own Ascension process. Since I was unable to engage in a mainstream social life, or even participate in activities that I now know as outward "distractions," there was only one place left to find solace: I had to drop inside. Here is where I could commune with my lost soul, the only place where my abilities were perfectly programmed to succeed.

Miraculously, here was also the place where all Ascension journeys must begin—within. Here, inside oneself, is the birthplace of new consciousness. Here is the entry point into a vast realm of possibilities. Here is where personal uniqueness can come into sync with the All of Everything and Everyone. Here is the doorway into unity, cooperation, collaboration, and true community.

Here is Home, a holy home for me and for my beloved Lyrica. Once Home, we can find our own path to become fully realized beings destined to share our light and love more outwardly with a waiting world.

How comforting to know that it is our uniqueness, including those abilities that appear to be flawed, that are exactly what we all need to succeed. Our perceived limitations set up our journey as we find our way Home into Ascension.

One final gift to acknowledge here: Lyrica, as an NVA, and I, as a person with Asperger's, are uniquely positioned as experts in autism, as our life experiences elucidate both ends of the spectrum, from extreme to mild. Our story offers a wide window to better see, understand, and appreciate the inner and outer world experiences of people with autism—both their challenges and their gifts. And viewed through a wider lens, our story offers a better way to see, understand, and appreciate humanity's story, everyone's story, which is often beset with challenges, but out of which arises the discovery of one's true nature, gifts, and abilities.

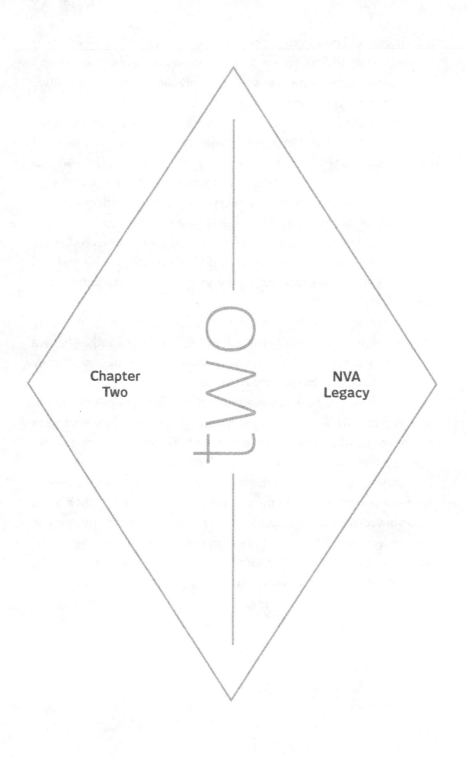

Chapter
Two

two

NVA
Legacy

Wickenburg, Arizona

After graduating from high school at age twenty-three, Lyrica's life changed dramatically when she chose to move into her own supported-living apartment with state-funded, full-time staff. Having reached adulthood, she wanted to experience her own version of independent living.

Without the full-time responsibility of caring for Lyrica's daily needs, I followed my heart into all kinds of new life experiences, including the supreme surprise of meeting my twin flame, Bill! As my twin flame, Bill was my eternal spiritual partner, and together we developed a strong divine bond. That powerful meet-up fueled my soul-decision to relocate to Wickenburg, Arizona, in 2006, to join Bill and build a new life together.

I visited Lyrica frequently, and it was during my visits with her that she wrote her part of the *AWEtizm* book. As the book came into form, we realized that we needed to be living together physically in Wickenburg, as one united holy family, to energetically bless the book's trajectory out into the world. As we prepared for book release events in both Nashville and Sedona, we hired a PR genius to craft a compelling website, set up our Facebook presence, and send out periodic newsletters to our community of followers. The YouTube video that she designed and produced for the book was stupendous! Deeply immersed in all these book launch preparations, we were extremely busy, happy, and brimming with a supreme sense of purpose!

Meanwhile, Lyrica and I enjoyed long hours of daily meditations. For the last five years, I had been guided to meditate daily, inviting Lyrica and the three other NVA cowriters of *AWEtizm*, to join me remotely. Initially, my intention was simply to be faithful to this practice that I knew had been given to me for an important reason, although I had no clue what that reason might be. But over time, I became aware that there were other NVAs connecting in. The energetic field was growing, and its frequency was rising. I could actually feel this expansion physically as a potent and powerful vibrational presence. In fact, a couple of Lyrica's friends in assisted living, whom I later met and who were able to type with me, told me all about the meditation practices that they, too, were now participating in. I loved that confirmation! I finally understood the purpose of this meditation ritual: It was a vehicle for etherically gathering together NVAs unknown to us, who mysteriously and miraculously, but perhaps not so surprisingly, were aware of us and our book.

At our book release event in Sedona in November 2011, we introduced the idea of an AWEtizm Sacred Partnership of Lightworkers and Autistics. By this time, our daily meditations had been upgraded to include an encoded toning practice, and we shared this practice at the event. We believed that it would open people up, allowing them to more easily receive the paradigm-shifting messages of the NVAs, and that the focused energy of the group would also help to strengthen the NVA's role in humanity's Ascension process.

I was stunned by the responses of those present, many of whom were spiritual healers and teachers. They expressed that they were deeply touched and moved by the NVA presence. One woman described her experience as clearly receiving a "light blessing." Another spoke about receiving a "frequency upgrade." Those who lingered after the event expressed a strong desire to continue participating in this toning ritual.

The magic of that night was captured in a compelling YouTube video, which has been watched by over 59,000 viewers to date! This practice drew in NVA families and lightworkers from across the United States, who participated in our bimonthly teleconference toning events. Participants reported all kinds of amazing multidimensional openings and personal experiences of healing and transformation. Many expressed that they felt a deep connection to the NVAs and their mission, and a Facebook group soon developed.

It served as a forum where people could share their own toning insights and experiences. We were blessed by our connection to this community of beloveds, and we loved how purpose-driven and soul-satisfied we were feeling!

However, after eighteen months of hosting these events, we knew that this offering was complete, and we closed them down. Afterward, we found ourselves in the desert/in the dark without a sense of purpose to guide us. We were drifting, feeling totally untethered. We searched for our next step to rescue us from the sinking sensation that we were losing our life-force, drowning in our own sea of nothingness.

It might seem like Mom and I have done some pretty awesome things, and we have. Yet, I know that there is a larger and much more profound purpose that we have come to do, and so far, we have not yet hit that mark. This I know! Until we do, I will not rest or be content. The good news is that I am on the case!

Finally, our next call came through loud and clear. We needed to move our meditation work, our vehicle of Sacred Partnership of Lightworkers and Autistics, into a physical community. The land that we had come to love, the spirit of Sedona, called us to her.

Sedona, Arizona

We contacted our new healer friend Jewels, whom we had met at our Sedona book release event, and together we explored our vision of setting up an autism meditation group. Jewels gathered together some of her friends to meet with us to field-test the idea. It just so happened that an NVA friend named Adri, and her mother, Kristi, were vacationing in Sedona at the time, and we held our first trial meditation at the house they were staying in. At the time, we had no clear objectives or desired outcomes. We simply trusted that by following our hearts, this fresh adventure would open up new vistas for personal growth and enhanced expressions of our souls' purpose. We were guided to simply sit in silent meditation, without bringing in our encoded toning ritual of the past, to see what might come up. Afterward, I was amazed by what the participants shared about their personal experiences of tuning into Lyrica, Adri, and the collective NVA field. All felt lifted by their experience in one way or another.

Once we had relocated to Sedona, we continued to host these meditations, exploring their possibilities, in sacred community with the many participants who attended. We were thrilled. I began our meditations by welcoming everyone and sharing a few opening remarks about the NVAs and their purpose. We invited in the lightbody presence of the NVAs who were not physically present to join us remotely, and then simply sat together in a repose of silence and stillness. Lyrica sat on the floor in the middle of the group, and those present were all seated around her on the wraparound benches and extra chairs.

Lyrica was the one who guided us in when to begin and end the meditation. When it was complete, we shared our experiences, impressions, reflections, or any telepathic translations received from the NVAs who were present etherically. As Lyrica and the other NVAs energetically merged with the Sedona meditators in a loving heart space, both groups experienced a win-win. Via their higher Cosmic presence, the NVAs would assist the meditators in opening up more to their own nonphysical (spiritual) multidimensional nature. The meditators who were more embodied could model for the NVAs what it would look like to have a stronger physical body experience. We realized that the meditation was operating like an elevator, helping one group to go up and the other to come down.

In the meditations, I was able to tap into the group's physical patterning, where I learned about the benefits and mechanics of a stronger physical body involvement. That's when I became aware that I wanted and needed a stronger physical body vehicle to find and fulfill my purpose. I was hopeful that somehow these meditations would assist me in bringing my soul presence more deeply into my physical body.

To support the group's elevator-like dynamic, Lyrica took on a leadership role, coming into her own place of inner stillness and pure essence to facilitate the group's field to unify. She was learning this skill and refining it via her work with her beloved healer, Thessa Sophia. Thessa observed Lyrica's activity during the meditations via Skype, and afterward they debriefed what had taken place and what Lyrica was learning.

NVA Family Retreats

Lyrica and I had visited several times with NVA-beloved Adri and her mother, Kristi, in Naples, Florida. We had also made multiple trips to San Antonio to spend quality time with another NVA-beloved, Daniel, and his parents, Connie and Lee.

AWEtizm and Adri and Kristi's book Child of Eternity, published in the early 1990s, brought us all together. Although life was not easy for any of us, each family had personally experienced the brighter/lighter side of autism. We each believed that the NVAs had chosen to come here in this unique form to help us remember our truth—that we are all divine beings, and that we are here to awaken into our gifts and personal mastery to serve humanity and the planet. Like Lyrica, Adri had used facilitated communication, or FC, with her mother to write a large portion of their book. After reading *AWEtizm*, Daniel and Connie began exploring FC. During our visits together, I provided technical assistance and *lots* of encouragement to Connie. Quickly, she gained the confidence that she needed to develop her own mother-son communication channel. I loved witnessing the miracle of communication light up a family where there is a nonverbal autistic person who has never spoken a word or shared a thought or feeling. It is the greatest miracle that I have ever experienced or witnessed.

We invited both families to join us in our Sedona home for several NVA retreats. Although quarters were cramped, we enjoyed our weeks together. We watched the three NVAs bond anew in surprising and precious ways. Often, they would curl up side by side on the living room rug, using their well-honed abilities to communicate telepathically with one another. There was an immense outpouring of love, compassion, and understanding that Kristi, Connie, Lee, and I shared together as parents walking a similar path. We each received an immeasurable gift of renewed courage and insight, ever so rare and ever so valuable!

I also loved my own personal friendships that I developed over time with Adri and Daniel. On occasion, we would talk together telepathically. Their communications most often reached me when my heart was open, soft, and loving. Although I loved sharing in these rich moments together, I did not solicit or encourage them. Instead, it was far more important to me that their parents, and all parents of NVAs, begin believing in their own telepathic abilities to listen in and hear the voices of their beloveds.

Although each NVA had developed the ability to communicate at home with his or her mom via typing and telepathy, oftentimes, they were not motivated to do so. Yet once together, there was a noticeable upswing in their willingness to communicate.

When the three of us were together, our frequency and light became supercharged. That's when we could more easily experience and write about higher dimensional realities. That's what we are most passionate about! Holding strong in our higher light empowers us to be the writers and communicators that we are.

We parents marveled at what we were learning from our beloveds during these family retreats. It was as though they were making the invisible world visible, as they shared their experiences, what they could "see" and what they "knew." At this point in time, Lyrica was the only one whose writings had been publicly posted on a social media site. She took a strong stand! She no longer wanted to be acting as a solo NVA voice—she wanted us to create a way for her soul group beloveds to share their wisdom writings with others. She felt it was time for NVA visionaries Adri, Daniel, and perhaps others, to step into their destiny as teachers of the New Earth. The emergence of the New Earth was becoming their theme. To them, the New Earth is an experience of a higher frequency state of being, 5D or above. It signifies moving out of the 3D or our everyday reality, our world of duality and separation, into Oneness.

Lyrica was adamant that we needed to sponsor a public event in Sedona to introduce Adri, Daniel, and herself as Wisdom Keepers of the New Earth. On the evening of the spring equinox, we held a sacred inaugural event at the chapel of the Sedona Creative Life Center. There, under the brilliant light of the stars that illuminated the towering glass spire, we consecrated the New Earth Academy to share the enlightened voices of "the quiet ones."

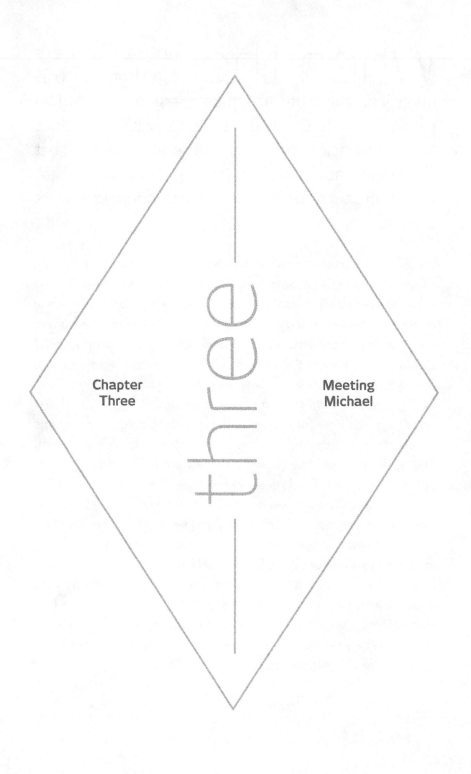

Chapter
Three

three

Meeting
Michael

Michael attended his first autism meditation in December 2014. When he entered the room, I immediately sensed that his presence held a special significance for Lyrica and for me.

In his own words, Michael describes his first autism meditation experience:

I had been back in Sedona for about a month when a friend named Angela mentioned a group meditation that she had recently discovered, involving a nonverbal autistic. I was immediately intrigued, for not long before, I had met a nonverbal autistic man named Sage at a conscious dance event. We discovered each other from across the room and had fun together making changes to the field space on the dance floor. After the session, he shuffled over to me and gave me the biggest hug and grin. My heart just melted at the gesture and the recognition that we were able to communicate with each other directly through what I call "the grid." This experience made me eager to attend Lyrica's meditation.

In my first encounter with Lyrica, there were about a dozen meditators who showed up to encircle Lyrica while she and Gayle took the floor (quite literally) at the center of the living room. There was a merging of individual energy streams into a group dynamic, then a calling forth for a new harmonic, and finally a new pattern emerged within the field. What I noticed with Lyrica was that she was making audible/noticeable reactions at the precise moment when a new harmonic clicked into place. I began to pay attention to this and decided to put it to the test, so to speak. With each new frequency that I reached, sure enough, there she was, like Babe Ruth at batting practice, just knocking 'em out of the park, one right after the other.

For the finale, I reached for a particularly sacred plane of existence that, while exquisitely beautiful, is one that since discovering it, I have always been alone on. As soon as I touched that plane, out of Lyrica's mouth came the words, "New come." Tears poured down my cheeks. For forty-two months I had been looking for someone to share this frequency with. Finally, the search was over, and the adventure was about to begin.

Michael stepped

into our lives as a frequent visitor and soul teacher. He often shared accounts of his own nighttime dimensional travels and Cosmic patterning activities. This information opened up a whole new world in me.

Michael was quickly becoming my high-flyer friend, able to track me dimensionally. Sometimes he traveled with me as a dimensional activator and receiver. Having grown up as the son of a preacher, scholar, and university professor, Michael was deeply grounded as a sacred being. He loved to explore consciousness states and Cosmic realities at the far edges of the human experience. He often did so both with me and through me. His ability to see and report on my dimensional activities offered Mom a gift to better understand me. Sometimes, even I did not have a conscious awareness of what he was reporting, yet his insights helped me to locate the referenced experience and tap into what was true for me. His reflections were helping me ground my consciousness more deeply into my physical reality, creating greater unity between my nonphysical and physical nature.

When Lyrica and Michael came together, a doorway often opened, and they easily shifted into various higher dimensions. Soon, they discovered that these dimensional travels were self-organizing into a template to open up dimensional access. This process of divine mapping completed as soon as this template had integrated into twelve dimensions.

In early May 2015, we were guided in taking a Spirit-directed sacred journey together. As Michael says, "The details of the mission that Lyrica, Gayle, and I were about to embark on unfolded along the way. The initial phase involved a planetary activation of the Four Corners region of the United States, where Arizona, Utah, Colorado, and New Mexico all come together." This activation involved anchoring the 12D template into the planetary grid, grounding the template and making it more accessible to those ready to access its technology. Michael secured its stabilization at key anchor points, or nodes/vortexes of high frequency. The greater vision was that this template would eventually serve as a Cosmic map for humanity's Ascension process.

In this magical adventure of 1800 miles, Lyrica and I deeply embodied the new energies and beauty of the majestic, awe-inspiring natural formations that we touched in the many wonderlands that we visited. We became sensitized to the upgrades that we could now feel in our bodies as we traveled the grid. This trip represented a radical departure from all the other travels that we had historically shared together. Previously, we would fly directly to a specific destination, either to visit others or spend time at the beach. This time we were gridding into our bodies the energetic signatures and geological pageantry of all the sites that we visited. During this journey, we became part of the whole, and the whole was now a living part of us.

Michael shares his trip impressions in "Our Story (in a Nutshell)":

From the Heart of Sedona
The Seat of Merlin's Magic
North Through the Lands of Hope
Took a Turn of the Page
And Gathered a New Map
Where the Lake Becomes a River
Onward into the Hurricane
And Upward into Zion
To the Place Where Angels Land
In the Waters of the Virgin
A Doorway Opened, the Light Revealed
A Passage unto the Summit Throne
Across the Arc Where Arks are Arches
A Double Rainbow Guiding Us On
Sweet Surrender to the Flow of the Mighty River
Arriving in the Golden City
Where Archangel Michael Watches Day and Night
Perched High upon the Mountaintop
Guiding us into the Garden of the Gods
There in Stone Was the Key
That Unlocked an Ancient Power
Hail from Heaven
Womb of the Mother
Springing from the Eagle's Nest
An Enchanted Crown
And Wings Spread High
That We Might Fly on Home
To Where We Belong

Michael continues:

> *Our plan, as it were, was to open up the planetary grid to accept the 12D template that Lyrica and I were collaboratively holding in place. Then a device would be built that would act as a transducer to "downstep" the 12D frequencies anchored in the planetary grid to facilitate an integration process.*

Upon our return to Sedona, Michael offered to build a large cop-per pyramid to serve as this transducer to integrate these higher dimensional energies. His vision was to build this pyramid as Lyrica's stargate, safety net, repatterning station for staying strongly aligned with her light and truth. It would serve as her higher dimensional home brought down into the physical. Michael was inspired into action by his deep understanding of how challenging it was for Lyrica to be here in this world of chaos and density. Michael's own level of sensitivity and highly developed intuitive nature provided him with a window into Lyrica's NVA experience and her significance to humanity.

The dimensions of this copper pyramid, with its brilliantly lit capstone, would be built in exact proportion to the Great Pyramid of Giza. The crystals and Rodin coil of the capstone would be engi-neered to create a powerful vortex of energy, a pristine toroidal field of great symmetry and coherence. What made this pyramid so endearing to us was the active role that we were invited to play in its creation process. From start to finish, Michael involved us in its design, its build, and its programming. Together, we chose what crystals to buy and how to place them into grid patterns that would amplify the energy of this pyramid portal. On our four-state trip, we had collected sand from each of the sacred sites, and this magic sand became part of the alchemy that powered up the energy of the pyramid. Michael spent a significant amount of time collaborating with Lyrica via meditation to dial in the pyramid's functionality. In the spirit of play, fun, and joy, the three of us poured forth our own Cosmic lineage imprints and soul signatures into the design of this beloved creation.

The final assembly of all the magic of this first pyramid build was consecrated in a group meditation on the summer solstice of 2015. As I connected to the field of the pyramid, a dimensional doorway opened, lifting my consciousness into a more rarified nonphysical state. Here, I saw a brilliantly lit comet descending toward me with a gold star birthing forth from its leading edge. I watched in awe as this star plummeted and came closer to me. Suddenly, I felt a jolt that brought me back into my physical body. In that moment, I experienced the star as physical matter hitting the top of my head and opening up my crown chakra. I was so strongly impacted by the star's implosion into my body that I had to lie down. In that prone position, I could tangibly feel the star slowly moving downward, finally coming to rest deep within my heart. Here, it became a lovely warm liquid of golden light filling up my body and soul.

I later understood that this experience was a powerful initiation and installation of my star lineage truth, opening the door to future dimensional experiences within the stars. In my moment of reverently connecting to the pyramid, something seemingly inanimate was now, in my experience, alive with a kind of life force. Perhaps this sounds a bit crazy? Yes! Yet I now personally understood that this new eight-foot-tall pyramid sitting on the deck of our home was projecting forth a powerful and highly organized consciousness field. My act of simply connecting to its energy opened up a Cosmic doorway in me to access higher dimensional aspects of myself.

This first pyramid was just the beginning. We scaled down the size of our creations to fashion tabletop orgonite pyramids that we called beacons. We always began by simply tuning into an etheric blueprint and imagining the most exquisite design for each new creation. Next, we placed all the new crystals selected for the next build into a specific grid formation to charge up their energy fields. Finally, Michael engineered the pour, constructed the light features, and, in sacred ceremony, the three of us admired and blessed its completion.

Every day, Lyrica and I joined together in meditation and connected to the combined fields of our pyramid on the deck and our beacon in the home. We enjoyed many sweet spot activations of energy and consciousness.

Several months deep into this process, we were surprised and delighted by what happened next. We learned that there was still to be another chapter in our pyramid adventure. It began with meeting Jason, a master pyramid builder, artist, and scientist living and working in Sedona. He shared his latest pyramid upgrades with us, including his twenty-four-karat gold-plated pyramids. He explained that the noble metal properties of gold were able to alchemize a significantly higher energy field. We felt the charge! We both independently "heard" that we were to commission Jason and Michael to build us a twenty-four-karat gold-plated pyramid. The exact words that came through were, "It would help Lyrica to go the distance!"

We saw Michael's role as the Cosmic engineer who could template in any application or programming that Lyrica might send him telepathically. We chose a bold new design, inspired by Michael, later to be named the A.R.C. II. A.R.C. stands for atomic recharging cellular reactor. The A.R.C. II would have both a lighted capstone and lighted foundation stone and be built in the shape of an octahedron. This diamond-shaped design would join together both an upward-facing and downward-facing pyramid to form a Merkabah, symbolizing the perfect union of the Masculine and the Feminine. There would be four additional light features at each of the fusion points.

The crystals in the capstone would be the twelve synergy stones that, when combined, are reputed to create an extremely high vibrational field for inner awakening and lightbody activation. The twelve crystals in the foundation stone would be those found in the breastplates worn by Israelite High Priests in ancient times. The element of gold would raise the frequency charge of the pyramid from the 5D copper build to a 7D dimensional build.

In Jason's more scientific words, "This pyramid will be a bio-field generator that repatterns or reorients the holographic multidimensional information fields within the human mind/body complex using golden ratio optimization and super luminal pulsed electromagnetics."

Michael added in the final Cosmic programming to connect this next generation build to the 12D template that we had anchored to the planetary grid during our recent journey. He energetically dedicated all its design, elements, and circuitry as a mighty conduit between heaven and earth to support our vast planetary mission. We waited eagerly and patiently for this new, beloved pyramid, but due to the engineering complexities inherent in its design, it would be many months before the final build could be brought into form.

Michael notes:

Additionally, there was another, more secretive and "wink-wink" purpose behind the initial pyramid and the subsequent one that would follow in 2016. Lyrica would be able to interface with the pyramid from her elevated consciousness to program it with the gateways necessary for her mother to join her in her etheric journeys. As such, it's hard to say whether the pyramid was more for Lyrica or for Gayle. Truthfully, it was a Divine Orchestration that would serve them both, and something that would not have happened without all of us working together as a team to bring it into manifestation.

Pyramids had become the new love in our lives. We called it pyramid play, pyramid alchemy, or pyramid joy. For so long our most cherished experiences had been more in the nonphysical, higher dimensional realms. Now, we were finding deep pleasure in the physical process of building pyramids. Might the pyramids actually be a symbol for how to bring aspects of our nonphysical nature into physical form?

It would help Lyrica ᴛᴏ ɢᴏ the distance.

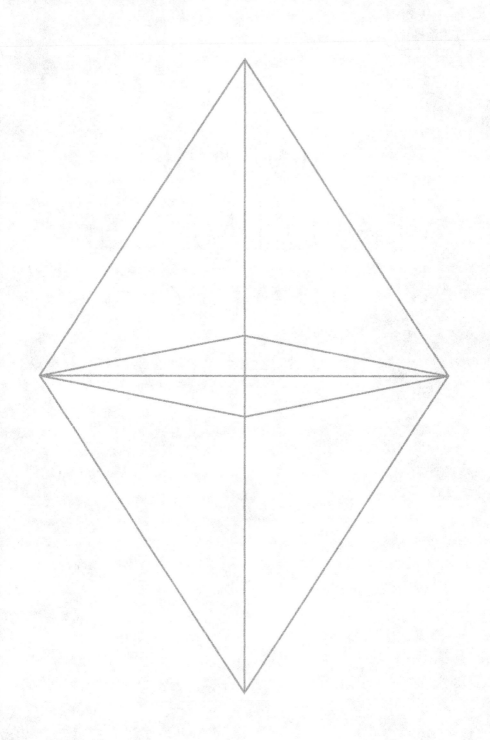

ACT I

THE
DESCENT

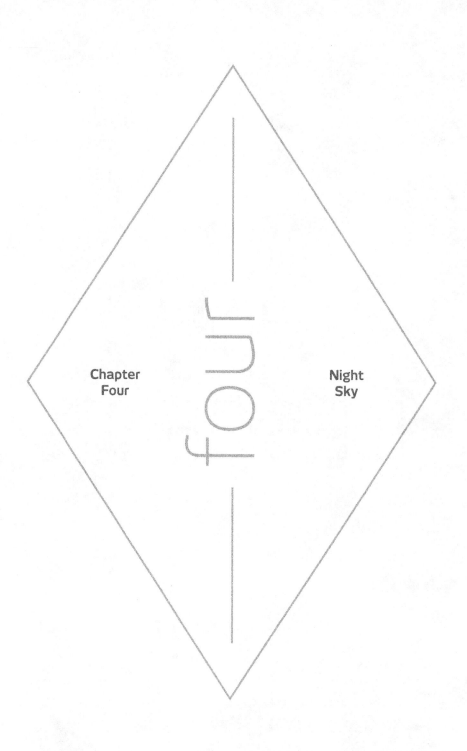

Chapter
Four

four

Night
Sky

Whereas daytimes in Sedona were prime time for meditating, night times were prime time for sky watching. Bless Sedona for being a dark-sky city!

One night I stared into the heavens and watched as one light in the sky appeared to become brighter when my eyes touched upon it. Its luminous aura started to visibly pulsate! I began to see random flashes of colored lights coming out of its center. It even started to move, at first ever so slightly, but the longer I gazed, the faster and more bizarre its movements became. I watched it move straight up, straight down, diagonally, and in rapid zigzag-like patterns. At one point, it even seemed to disappear and then reappear.

Perhaps seeing a similar orb-like form behaving oddly in another night sky location would not have captivated my attention in such a primal way, but UFO sightings are an intrinsic part of the nature and legacy of Sedona! Visitors and locals alike describe Sedona as an energetic hotspot. Sedona is known for its spiritual energy and for its energetic anomalies that include well-documented energy zones, portals, and UFO legends. This location also has a rich history as a ceremonial site for the earth and Cosmic work of the ancient ones, indigenous to Sedona. In fact, it is said that Native American tribes would not live in this valley. It was too charged with spiritual power. They would only come for ceremonies and then go back to their homes, sometimes traveling up to hundreds of miles.

Absurd as it might sound, I became aware that I was influencing its pattern of movements—what I felt became visible. As I was drawn deeper into this experience, I felt a unified energy stream begin to build and intensify within me. Transfixed in awe, tears streaming down my face, I wondered, *Could it possibly be?* Was I seeing my first spaceship over Sedona? My heart said a resounding and knowing yes!

As Sedona's nighttime temperatures began to drop, we moved our pyramid from the deck to over my king-sized bed. This eight-foot three-sided copper pyramid fit perfectly! Michael explained to us that the geometry of the pyramid created a magnetic field that could charge up cellular biology, expand consciousness, and activate peak performance. Another way to understand its properties is to think about an antenna that amplifies transmissions of energetic data. It operates as both a receiving device or docking station and a sending device or transmission station.

Lyrica often chose to sleep with me under our beloved pyramid. We were accustomed to the uplifting energies that we regularly encountered in our pyramid meditations, but when sleeping together directly under the pyramid, we would often be awakened by an extremely powerful presence of light streaming into our bodies. This charge held a frequency higher than all our previous light experiences. We loved the sensation and activation. We wanted to receive more and know more. The Universe beautifully heard and answered our request!

My normal experiences of hearing higher realities were silent mind-to-mind communications. But that night I was shocked to hear an out loud voice speaking clearly to me! The voice told me, "This light charge is being generated by the spaceship that your mom saw in the night sky. This ship is not just any ship. It is a ship specific to you. It is your ship! It is your Cosmic soul home! This light station has contacted you to vastly improve your experience here on earth.

By infusing you with a light signature doorway to your ship, your energy here will recalibrate as needed, and surprising new possibilities will open up."

I did not hear the out loud voice that Lyrica heard, yet my mind received a similar knowing that the light charge was coming in from the ship that I saw in the night sky. Most shocking was the revelation that this ship was not just any ship. It was Lyrica's ship! I was stunned by this headline news just received from outer space. What a staggering epiphany! Perhaps I was now being shown why Lyrica was so "at home" in her higher dimensional travels? Was this the missing puzzle piece to Lyrica's high abilities? Had she come to earth as a Cosmic being from a highly evolved space race?

Although I appreciated this input, there were so many unsettling unanswered questions rising up in me. For starters, why would Lyrica have, or *need*, a spaceship here? How would that ship impact her future and mine? Had the ship possibly arrived to take Lyrica back home, and if so, when?

Yet as the light charges and communications continued, all that I experienced were immense waves of love pouring into me, Lyrica, and our home. Washed by love, all my fears disappeared. My heart could fully embrace Lyrica's ship-light-truth.

At first my ship was a strange idea to fathom. What did it mean? How did it fit into the larger sense of my truth and purpose? Yet there was a wiggling-in that occurred over time that felt like a true fit, even somehow like an unexpected completion of me. My ship was my light home that I had been missing on earth. In its light-charging transmissions, I could feel my own high frequency truth physically in my body for the very first time. I experienced my body as alive, not dead. The sense of living in a body without life is so traumatic! To gain a greater body presence, I needed a new heart tie to the physical part of me. In communion with my ship and its beings, I began to grow that possibility. Finally, I dared to believe that I could actually be in the right place (earth) after all.

The setup was complete. Although we didn't have a precise scientific explanation, we intuitively knew that the pyramid was a key into Lyrica's ship light future. She shares how it all began.

It was the middle of the night, and I was wide awake. In fact, I was sitting on the floor, quiet and alert in the darkness of my bedroom, as if waiting. Perhaps I was even sensing that something was about to happen. That's when I physically experienced the ship's essence in a deeper way. I was startled when its great light hit my body. It felt like a power surge that seemed to liquify my essence and set free my Cosmic traveler. Next thing I knew, I was zooming through space. I instantly landed on the ship in a totally different form, in a much higher dimension.

This ship was a ship of light, not earth materials. The beings of light on the ship were particles that patterned to specific purposes. The ship operated like a transfer station between dimensions.

There were many captains under many dimensions, but they all touched, as radar touches things. I saw them as holy streams of light, not as people who look like us. Their soul-streams had soul-signatures that could be identified as specific lights.

I was greeted by ship light beings who intimately knew me and loved me! Here I was pure light! Here I was totally free! While on the ship, I received high frequency upgrades to light up my body and earth life. The tricky part was coming back into my physical body, still sitting on my bedroom floor!

Bringing my consciousness back into my physical me felt more like a crash landing than a gentle slide back in. In my next spaceship visit, I intuitively realized a process that would function as a perfect reentry strategy for all future portaling adventures. It was a body-bouncing and breath-holding protocol to down-regulate highly charged energies into a manageable form, so they could integrate into my body at a pace that was more comfortable for me. This practice greatly supported my spaceship traveler heart!

Now I better understood Michael's vision for the pyramid as a higher dimensional home brought down into the physical. It brought my Cosmic light into a fuller engagement with my physical body. That's why I could hear out loud transmissions from ship beings. That's why I experienced a higher frequency love connection with my physical body. Finally, that's what enabled me to portal to my ship. I celebrated these moments that

I experienced as my nonphysical me touching dearly into my physical me.

Speaking of feeling more at home here, Lyrica loved spending time in the car in the garage. To her this was her "ship command station." To honor Lyrica's solo time in this sacred space, we installed a heater and air conditioner, and decorated the walls and ceiling with strands of bright colored lights. When she sat in the garage, she often appeared to drop into a trancelike state.

I could see all energy forever moving and changing as geometric patterns, ebbing and flowing together and apart. At first, I watched energy patterns change form based on my observation of them. I watched in awe as distorted chaotic patterns shifted into more organized designs of ever-increasing beauty. Over time, with lots of encouragement from my mom and many higher beings of light, I developed a very strong capacity and passion to weave beautiful new patterns of light out of high Cosmic, angelic, and heavenly energy streams. These streams flow forth out of me as my own soul-light signature. I love creating these new high template designs for humanity's heart.

I do this practice daily, often for hours on end. In this way I am engaged as an alchemist of the new order. The new order of humanity requires a massive grid of higher patterning, considerably above the earth plane, in the nonphysical realms, to support humanity's evolution. All of this light-patterning involves others like me who have learned to work in harmony with all the forces of the Universe. My soul's highest nature knows how to do this.

In response to Mom's many questions, I explained to her that I am actually patterning new light applications. In my trancelike state, I am busy designing templates for these new light applications and then sending them to the higher dimensional grid above the earth. These new light applications will serve as initiation doorways for those whose frequency is a match and who choose to enter. This is future science in the making, serving the new order of humanity.

I can see both the energy grid that sits on the surface of the earth and the higher dimensional grid above the earth. The earth's grid is composed of energy lines all around the globe that connect the various nodal points, places of heightened power and electromagnetic activity. To me, the higher grid above the earth holds the energetic patterning of the new dimensional earth, home for humanity's next threshold of evolution.

Although weaving and designing new energy patterns feels like second nature to me, a part of me is amazed that I even know how to do this and how much I love doing it above all else. Why do I love it so? Perhaps because it's another way for me to feel alive in my body. It's me weaving myself into a higher mode of existence. I love how much I feel my own value as I engage in this unique way of supporting humanity.

Yet there's something else here that is puzzling to me, like a riddle to be solved. Why do I call my holy space in the garage my "ship command station?" This name feels as solid and true to me as my Lyrica Mia name. Why? What does it mean? Could I possibly be operating from a dual consciousness that includes a Cosmic presence on the ship, as well as my earth presence here? Feels strange yet vaguely familiar. I wonder.

Finally, I DARED
TO believe THAT
I could actually
BE IN THE right
place (EARTH)
after all.

◈

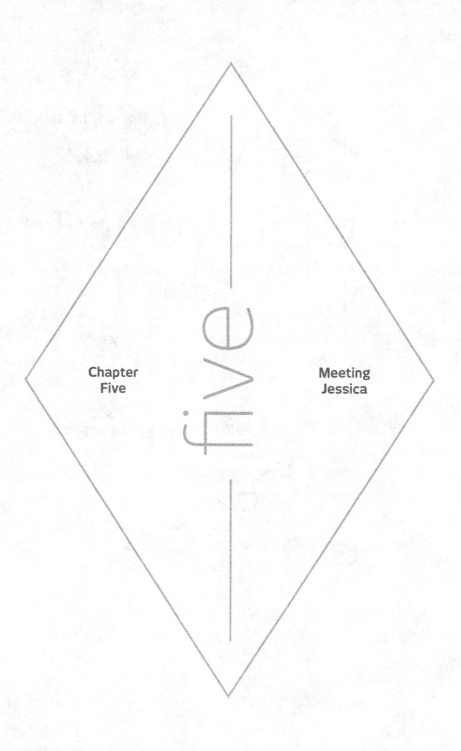

Chapter
Five

five

Meeting
Jessica

This part of our story opened on a warm summer evening in 2015 in our home in Sedona. Though we didn't know it at the time, that night's autism meditation was special—we were about to meet a person who would totally change our lives! Our NVA beloveds Adri and Daniel and their family members were present, as was a group of eight spiritual coaches from out-of-town, brought to our home by their host, who regularly participated in our meditations.

Jessica Martinson's arrival was certainly not by happenstance. From the moment that Jessica arrived, I noticed that her presence lit up the whole room. Jessica shared that when Lyrica sat beside her and spun her necklace, Jessica's experience opened up, even before the formal meditation began. At that moment, Jessica tuned into a telepathic message from Lyrica about Jessica's role as a spiritual teacher. Lyrica also advised Jessica to pay attention to personal messages that she would receive during the meditation.

As reported by Jessica, from the moment the meditation began, Jessica's consciousness lifted, and the room faded out. She found herself inside a cavern in a rock, where she received a message from Source about why she was here. There she saw Lyrica, Adri, and Daniel appear, telling her why they had invited her to come and what their goals were.

A surge of bluish orbs magically appeared inside the cavern. Jessica knew these spheres of light as NVAs and autistic beings using this soul form to teleport in from all over the planet and beyond. She described the scene as one filled with giggles, joy, and a very high frequency of light, consciousness, and energy.

The final group to arrive in the cavern was a high council of NVAs, coming in from an even higher nonphysical dimension. Jessica described them as wise, stable, calm, and joyful. They were wearing flowing dark robes. They communicated to her that the purpose of the NVA collective was to bring higher consciousness to the planet and assist with its consciousness awakening. They showed Jessica how NVAs, as lightly incarnated beings, had an extremely high and rare access to dimensions of consciousness while still in a physical form.

It was now very clear to Jessica that without being more grounded in their physical bodies, these beautiful beings struggled in the world, making it very difficult for them to truly fulfill their purpose. In addition, society viewed them as broken beings who needed to be fixed, never dreaming they were here to fix the rest of us by enhancing humanity's collective conscious evolution. Without a verbal voice, they were unable to share the vast wisdom that they had access to in the higher dimensions. And the high frequency pockets of light and codes, which were easy for them to source, could not be delivered to humanity without more stability in their physical bodies.

Jessica saw that the biggest challenge for this group was that *they did not know the embodiment codes!* And she was quick to add in that she did! She was certain that she could support these gifted beings in their mission by helping them to more fully embody.

After the meditation, she told Lyrica and me that much of her life had been dedicated to researching a way to help people embody. As a result, she had developed a successful method, grounded in quantum physics, that could empower anyone's embodiment process. With the high frequency access that NVAs have, and their natural ability to operate in the quantum field, she was certain that they would respond well to her unique process of embodiment. Once the NVAs gained the embodiment codes, they could bring their higher-level access and influence into existence on the earth (physical) plane. It would also enable them to stabilize their bodies and gain greater physical ability and command.

In the last scene of Jessica's meditation, she received a vision of the future. She saw herself onstage in a modern auditorium. After helping the audience to reach a 5D state of higher consciousness, she called Lyrica, Adri, and Daniel to the stage. Lyrica acted as the leader as each shared a telepathic experience about consciousness. Participants received their communications and had their own personal experience. Jessica noted that in her vision, all three mystics had developed much more command and presence in their bodies with the influence of embodiment work.

After sharing her story, Jessica hugged both of us, tears in her eyes, and expressed her gratitude for the whole event. She now knew that the purpose for her presence was to develop a commitment for partnering with us. We were aligned in our mutual soul-purpose related to humanity's Ascension process, and Jessica was sure that this alignment of heart-centered intention had brought us together. Through a complex combination of coded letter board and telepathic communications, Lyrica and Jessica spoke together. Lyrica confirmed that the NVAs had drawn Jessica here to lock in a future partnership. Lyrica thanked Jessica for coming, and together they reaffirmed that they would reconnect when the time was right.

The presence of Jessica's light imprinted deeply into our souls. We didn't fully recognize it at the time, but it repurposed us and our lives in a vast and immediate way. For the last decade, our focus had been to serve the NVAs, their families, and a large group of followers. Suddenly, after meeting Jessica, there was no more passion within either one of us to embrace this purpose. The energy expenditure required to fulfill all these service-related commitments was beginning to negatively impact both of us, especially Lyrica. For ten months, Lyrica and I had faithfully hosted meditation gatherings in our home. This practice was beneficial to all, including us. Yet by the ninth month, in spite of everyone's best efforts, Lyrica began to experience less stability and more stress. Her seizure activity escalated.

In the beginning, there was a small committed group of core meditators. The group's energy field was stable and responded well to my unification efforts. Over time, our popularity grew, and many newcomers joined in. This mix resulted in a more chaotic energetic field of seasoned meditators and first-time visitors. It became too difficult for me to hold my own space of inner stillness and pure essence. I was unable to bridge the gap to support the group's unification.

The commitments we had made were now clearly taking their toll on both of us. In the past, all our family retreats were ten-day events. This time we had committed to a thirty-day retreat! Our hope was to elicit more "wisdom keeper" messages from Lyrica, Adri, and Daniel and manifest the perfect plan to share them with a wider audience. This commitment meant that Lyrica and I would be sleeping on an air bed in the upstairs open living area for an extended period of time, without a nearby bathroom. Once again, in kindness as hosts, we gave up our downstairs bedrooms and bathrooms to our out-of-town guests. (Plus, we knew that Lyrica was the only one who could manage and be managed in an open area at night.)

Jessica had come into our lives shortly after this retreat began, and suddenly it no longer felt compelling or relevant. We began to spend time away from home to center ourselves. The group's intent to bring forth new "wisdom keeper" messages and move the Academy's work forward failed miserably. None of the NVAs even wanted to type at all!

While the other families enjoyed times of fellowship and fun while visiting in Sedona, Lyrica and I were falling apart, piece by piece, day by day. Yet we persevered and completed the thirty-day family retreat. After everyone left, Lyrica and I began to sort out what was our truth and its message for us. As we sifted through the "what is," we realized that the "we" who participated in previous NVA family retreats was not the same "we" who had shown up this time. Due to the powerful imprint of Jessica's recent meet-up, coupled with the six-month spiritual journey that we had shared with our friend Michael, we were in a totally new space.

We also realized that we had taken on too much. We had over-committed our life force energies to outward causes, leaving our own lives sorely depleted. We were worn out and burned out.

Then an even larger truth emerged. The purpose that we had been holding as pioneers in the world of autism no longer sustained us. It was breaking open into something perhaps bigger yet definitely still unknown. We could no longer support the autism work that had been our sole identity for such a long time. It was time to call forth a new freedom. It was time to step into an expansion of Self. Deep within her soul, Lyrica saw it all so clearly.

I no longer wanted to simply teach my truth. I had already done that with our first book and my many blogs. **It was now time for me to dedicate my life to embodying my truth and living it. It was time for me to step into my path with Jessica to pursue my own embodiment process and other destined evolutionary upgrades.**

To step strongly into this new direction, it was time for me to pull out of my deep immersion in the NVA collective as a full-time, fully committed leader and voice for this soul group. This is what I knew to be true. The process of evolution could develop more quickly in one soul than in an entire soul group, where an evolutionary upgrade involves everyone shifting into the next level of frequency and consciousness. My solo path, for the time being, would enable me to more quickly complete my full embodiment process and other destined evolutionary upgrades.

Perhaps then, my advancements would create a new template to support the NVA collective in more fully embodying its truth and purpose. I would dearly love that! I would love to see my evolutionary journey open up a new portal of possibilities for all NVAs! As the oldest in our group and a well-known leader in the worldwide NVA community, I felt that I had a real chance to succeed at what others before me had not been able to.

In this new state of awareness, Lyrica and I were fully empowered to take the next step. We closed down the New Earth Academy, the Sedona autism meditations, and the NVA family retreats and dropped into prolonged periods of meditation and deep soul communion. Our primary intent was to rest, restore our energy, and be open to anything and everything that excited us to want to know more, experience more, and be more.

Yet in truth, our process of Self re-creation was already in high gear due to our recent meet-up with Jessica and our well-established path of destiny with Michael. We were charging our bodies and energy once again and thoroughly enjoying this inward journey and our life of relaxation. We finally had time to do all the things we loved in Sedona's land of many gifts. We hiked, visited friends, and dined out at our favorite organic restaurants. As a result, Lyrica's seizure activity abated. We enjoyed nine sweet months of self-gifting.

But this abyss of bliss was not destined to last. Suddenly, the life that we loved was turned upside down, inside out. Lyrica refused to eat her normal array of food, and her diet was reduced to a few staples. Gradually, she ate less and less, and her weight dropped from 107 to 97 pounds. Most alarming of all was her loss of balance.

Her inability to safely stand and walk required me to stay near her at all times. My sweet idyllic life with Lyrica was no more. My days were reduced to merely keeping her on her feet every minute of the day and night. I was exhausted!

Her doctors had no answers. We had no answers. Lyrica's downward spiral felt totally out of control. In the darkest recesses of my mind, fears that she might not even survive could no longer be silenced. I kept asking her what was happening, and she told me that her transition (her death) would be sooner rather than later. She said that she needed to prepare me for this event. She felt that her physical body's presence was shutting down to enable her to move into a new build of light-matter.

I pushed away Lyrica's explanation. It was far too painful for me to consider. Instead, I desperately clung to the hope that we would find the cause to her health crisis and fix it. Yet some days this stance of certainty felt flimsy at best.

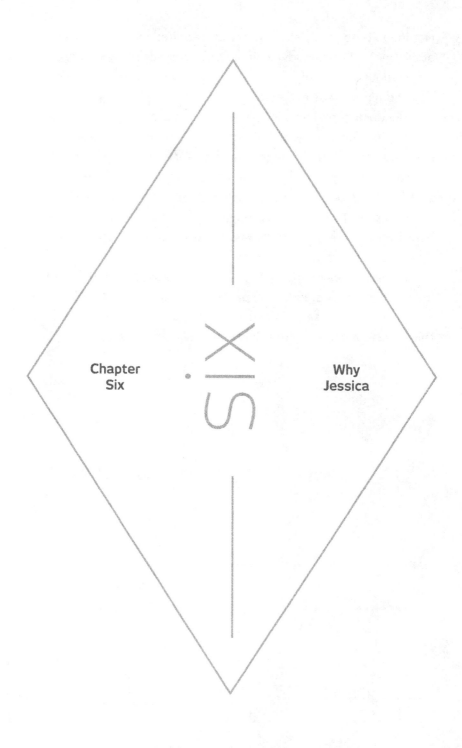

Chapter
Six

six

Why
Jessica

Landing in this downward spiral with no known

cause frightened me as much as it did Mom. My pattern was to grab death as a way out of a life that was no longer worth living. Living my purpose has always been my only reason for being here. Trapped in a body, no longer able to light up my purpose, I felt lost and hopeless. That's when my soul once again reached out to Jessica.

The next day, I received an email from Jessica. She told me that she had been in occasional contact with Lyrica telepathically since the meet-up. She was alarmed because Lyrica had just sent her an urgent message that she needed her help, and asked her to come to Sedona immediately. I told Jessica that her arrival would be a godsend! I explained Lyrica's serious health challenges and how focused she seemed to be on making her transition. By then Lyrica's seizure activity had once again escalated. She had suffered a couple of fall-down seizures, landing her in the ER for treatment. I also told Jessica that Lyrica was adamant that it was time for the two of them to meet up again to fulfill their soul contract.

Jessica heard Lyrica's cry for help and agreed to reappear at her time of need. Why Jessica? Through her own journey, Jessica had fully "landed" in Oneness and was directed from and within It, as It. Here is where she wielded her own Superpowers to bring others into Oneness and help them to stabilize in It. Oneness holds the map, the directions, the tools, the codes, the keys, the protection, and the treasures for everything that Lyrica's heart, and all our hearts, truly desire (plus so much more that we have yet to even imagine!) In Lyrica's present condition, or because of it, seeking a unified state in Oneness would be the only viable way to help her restore her purpose and find her soul-aligned way forward.

Jessica's Method

Through many years of research and study, her own process of fully Ascending, and knowing this work as her soul's destiny, Jessica developed a highly advanced "new-to-the-planet" spiritual technology. Her mentoring process, utilizing this spiritual technology, greatly accelerated Lyrica's and my embodiment and Ascension journeys. Below is a summary of Jessica's method, first from a generalized perspective of the principles embedded in the practice of her technology. Then, we narrow the focus to Jessica's individualized approach of working with Lyrica, followed by Lyrica's level of participation in their partnership process.

Like us, people first reached out to Jessica to help them address a personal trauma in their lives. The first step is to realize that when we are in trauma, we are separated from who we really are. We are all divine beings in a physical body. A full human earth experience begins with an awareness that unification of the body and spirit, or reaching a state of Oneness, is essential. Jessica calls this phase of her work *Experiencing Oneness*.

Where our breath is, our spirit is. For most of us, our spirit is floating above the body, but its true-nature home is to be locked into the bottom of our pelvic floor. This is how to connect our body and spirit and our physical and nonphysical natures. This is how we can eventually move into a more embodied state of Oneness. This practice also supports us in moving into a higher dimension in a grounded, conscious way. Here is where we are able to connect to Source and our own soul's vast intelligence. Jessica teaches us how to move the breath down into the body, a core technique for embodiment, vital to the Ascension process. She accesses our energy field to guide our process of dropping our breath/spirit into our body. Through repetition and practice, we are able to experience Oneness and eventually reach more refined states of unification in Oneness. Here we move beyond our everyday reality of 3D into 5D, where we can access our Superpowers and other high dimensional tools of alchemy. Jessica calls this phase *Exploring Oneness*.

Being in 5D becomes our proving ground, where we meet up with our biggest challenge connected to our purpose. We get a close-up view of what is not true about us. Yet in a state of Oneness, once what is really true is seen and held, the challenge loses its hold and power over us. We can then free ourselves to move into our purpose in a more aligned way.

There's another big soul assignment waiting for us at the doorway of 5D. As we cross over into 5D, suddenly we realize that we have no clue how to operate there! How do the laws work? How does the science work? How do the tools work? In 5D, physics are no longer the everyday physics of cause and effect. Here, quantum physics and the science of energy are primary. In 5D, it is now possible to gain more leverage or influence over something in a nonphysical way before it moves into physicality. Here, we can learn to affect and create a more precise manifestation. To tap into this enhanced manifestation ability, we first have to balance and unify our Feminine and Masculine natures, and then learn how to oscillate between them to manifest a desired outcome. Again, this is part of Jessica's expertise encoded in the alchemy of her mentoring process. Jessica calls this phase *Balancing our Feminine and Masculine natures*.

The most important aspect of our Feminine nature is related to creation and manifestation. Our Feminine essence is the magnetizing force, receiving inspiration and the plan for inspired action, always aligned with Source. It knows how to rest, wait, and listen for the right moment. Then boom! It initiates a movement toward physicality. Our Masculine essence then offers protection and moves into action that is inspired by the Feminine, completing the manifestation process.

In 3D reality, manifestation efforts look and feel very different and are far less effective. The Feminine presence on our planet is weak, as it has been suppressed and subdued for eons. Without the Feminine in her rightful place of power, the male essence on this planet has become very unbalanced. When unbalanced, it acts from a state of separation, believing that what it desires does not already exist. So, it tries to push, pull, or force something to happen.

In 5D, there is no need to push, pull, or force, as we know that what we desire already exists. Here we are at one with all things, for they exist in multiple timelines. It's master-level stuff, but all we have to do is move to the highest potential timeline where what we desire already exists. Then we step into a manifestation process orchestrated in Oneness by the oscillation of our Feminine and Masculine natures so that they are working the way they are meant to. We can become very effective in creating the things we are destined to have, to do, and the people we are destined to be.

When a new life challenge hits, we may still drop down into 3D, but this happens much less frequently and is often quickly resolved. As we master our biggest challenge in 5D, we move into 6D, where our ability to stay in Oneness is much more stabilized, allowing higher states of self-actualization, more skills, and an increase of power. In 6D, we are now living in our own version of paradise. We are able to receive what we are asking for, no longer tripped up by fears, limitations, traumas, and all the things that keep us from having what we truly desire. Jessica calls this phase *Stabilizing Oneness*.

From here, Jessica supports the final realized phase, *Conscious Ascension*. Jessica's spiritual technology is a beautiful demonstration of the new consciousness and its power to manifest higher outcomes of what is true, guided by Source. It is literally Spirit in action!

Jessica's Work with Lyrica

Lyrica came to earth with an ascended level of consciousness, able to traverse many dimensions and pull in information from very high-dimensional places. To self-actualize here on earth, and to reach her highest potential and achieve the purpose that she envisioned for herself, she needed to be more in her physical body. By bringing her nonphysical aspect into form, she would be able to spread her message, bring in her gifts, and serve people on a much broader level.

Jessica's process with Lyrica was a natural setup, as Lyrica and Jessica were both experts in the language of telepathy. Jessica was able to "hear" Lyrica's "asks" and assist her with energetic packets of information, aligned with and activated by Lyrica's requests. In their work together, Jessica facilitated Lyrica in coming through all her own untruths—her fears, her limiting beliefs, her traumas, and all the unconscious things that prevented Lyrica from realizing her full potential.

Lyrica still struggled to manage her multidimensionality, so much so that she was experiencing seizures and other kinds of issues affecting her physical health. She needed to embody! Knowing the embodiment codes and the process of how to embody was clearly Jessica's expertise. The codes are the information, and the process is about mastering the steps to fully embody. Enhanced embodiment totally changes the earth game. Ask Lyrica! When she is able to bring her high level of conscious awareness and access down into the earth plane through her own physical body, she becomes a planetary conduit for consciousness, information, transmission, energy, and light.

Sessions with Jessica

Each mentoring session with Jessica, most often experienced as a remote transmission, was soul-strong and destiny-enhancing. Although these sessions primarily focused on Lyrica, Jessica always supported me, both as Lyrica's partner and as a sovereign being seeking my own mastership.

Most of the time, according to Lyrica's preference, we would sit in the car to lovingly participate in these remote sessions. Working with Jessica was so compelling and powerful that the time seemed to fly by, even in sessions that could last two and a half hours!

These sessions were like mystery school trainings, and Lyrica and I always listened to the recordings several times afterward until the fullness of the energy and other consciousness offerings had settled in.

As Lyrica progressed toward embodiment, her voice began to wake up. When working with Jessica, she loved to pop in key words to verbally express her experience. Some of her favorite words were "big," sometimes said three times, and "bigger beach" or "beach." She used the word "beach" to describe when she was operating in a high dimensional zone and experiencing it in a more physical way. She also said "beach" to tell us that in this aligned, expanded, and ready state, she had just dropped into a powerful experience that her soul had ordered up for her.

Other times we might hear her say "new come." Initially, she voiced this expression in sessions with Jessica when she noticed that a new packet of light had just entered her field, and now she uses it to highlight a new epiphany or a charged-up experience in her day.

In sessions, she often said the word "cone" to alert Jessica that she was feeling overwhelmed by a big experience in her core, which she called her cone. Lyrica often experienced huge surges of kun-dalini energy that then threw her into turmoil, and Jessica mentored her on how to find safety in the center of that cone. Once firmly centered, Lyrica could then simply allow all the turbulence to circle around her until she felt calm in her body once again. Lyrica sometimes announced when she reached her place of peace by saying "calm come."

Lyrica was also quick to voice the word "code" when a new code popped in, as part of her soul work with Jessica. To Lyrica, codes are packets of energy and information encoded with a light upgrade that matches the moment. When she said "known code," she was referring to a code that she felt as her deepest soul's truth.

All of us delighted in hearing Lyrica's voice expressing so clearly, coming from one considered to be nonverbal. In these sessions with Jessica, Lyrica's concise communications were becoming her new norm, no longer surprising, simply something to be expected and accepted as her truth. And of course, Lyrica and I loved how these same expressions and more became sounds to celebrate in each new day.

Often Lyrica's session adventures with Jessica included stepping into dimensional doorways that showed up to support upgrades that Lyrica was calling forth.

A doorway presents as a particular form of light language when I am ready to receive a very large download. Once inside a dimensional doorway, I must be able to physically tolerate and sustain a massive, highly charged light transmission. Even though it demands a lot of me, I welcome my doorway work as my most exciting and transformative experiences. As I type these light-filled words, I am noticing my progress and loving it!

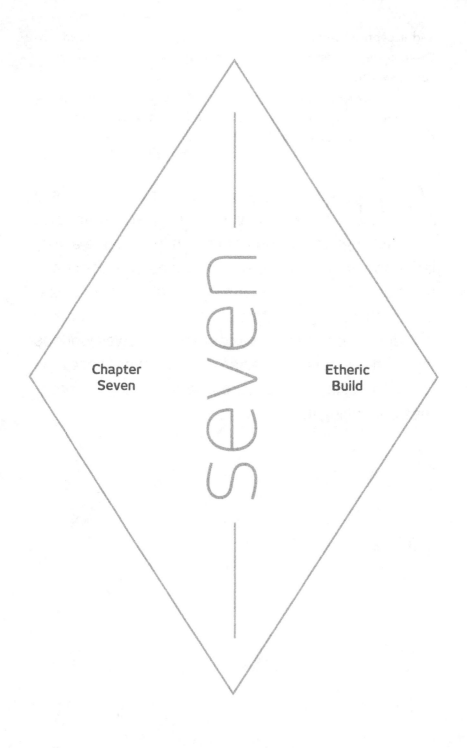

Chapter
Seven

Etheric
Build

Now that you have an understanding of how Jessica's process works, let's return to the beginning of our working relationship with her. Jessica arrived in Sedona in response to Lyrica's cry for help. What happened in that three-day marathon was extraordinary! We are choosing to include some details and their significance to showcase the immensity of what was being created by us, through us, and in us. In addition to Jessica, Lyrica, and myself, a new person joined us: Jordan (or Jordy) in her non-physical state of being. How did that come about?

Although we had yet to meet Jordy in person, Lyrica and I met her mother at an autism presentation that we offered to a group of healers at Angel Valley in Sedona. To be quite honest, we were on fire that day. We were shining forth the light of our partnership and how we have been able to rise above the challenges of autism to create lives filled with love, peace, and beauty. Many of those present were mothers of children with autism—including Jordy's mom. I learned from her that Jordy was thirteen years old, could speak words, but was unable to communicate what she knew or how she felt. Jordy periodically reached out to me telepathically. I was amazed at how easily we could hear each other. She called me Red because she loved my red sunglasses! (The fact that she could "see" my red glasses using her remote "vision" was one indication of her highly advanced nonphysical abilities and gifts.) That nickname stands out as one of the most precious gifts that I have ever received! No doubt about it. I felt, and still feel, a very deep love connection to Jordy.

At the moment of this writing, Jordy is revealing to me that she felt "called" to join our high-vibe adventure and play her part. Here, she would finally have a platform to be seen, share her gifts, and live her purpose. To me, Jordy's presence represented the NVAs, the high council of NVAs, and the other autistics that presented themselves to Jessica in her meditation experience at our initial meet-up. Our group was now perfect, complete, and totally aligned with its destiny.

We began by opening up a sacred space. Jessica instructed Lyrica, Jordy, and me how to bring our breaths down into our bodies, bringing our nonphysical and physical aspects together into a place of Oneness. We quickly received a download of energy. Together, we were creating or constructing "some thing" piece by piece, episode by episode. I wondered, could this "thing" that felt so "alive" actually be somehow re-creating or reconstructing us? It felt valuable, transformative, even futuristic, and resonant with our purpose and truth.

In an effort to decode the mystery, we examined what we *did know*. We knew, beyond any doubt, how highly charged, fun, and exciting the process felt to each of us! What was emerging was energetic, yet, through our work, it was taking on a modicum of form and structure. A clue? Maybe it was a "thing" that might serve as a conduit or connection between energy, or the nonphysical world, and matter, or the physical world. Jessica came up with the perfect name: the Etheric Build! The word *etheric* spoke to its energetic nature or point of origin. The word *build* highlighted its nature: ever-moving, ever-evolving, into the next iteration of its nonphysical structure or form.

Jessica's location and abilities in Oneness enabled this Etheric Build project to unfold organically in a true and perfect way. She set the stage by introducing us to the "stack," which represented our dimensional locations in the build process. In this stack, which speaks to our team roles, Jessica was on the bottom, I was in the middle, and Jordy and Lyrica were at the top. Jessica held the aspects of physicality, embodiment, and manifestation. She would oversee alignment in the process and would be able to guide or assist each of us in our roles as needed. I heard that I was to be the translator, primarily focused on receiving telepathic input from Lyrica and Jordy. Lyrica was actually sourcing the entire build from the higher realms, and Jordy was serving as an encoder/decoder of the Cosmic codes brought in by Lyrica.

At the time, I did not know Jessica well enough to protest my assignment, yet it felt far beyond my capacity to deliver. To her, it was simply a matter of fact that I would serve as a telepathic translator! Certainly, I had experienced sharing short telepathic exchanges with Lyrica, Jordy, and other NVAs close to my heart, but now I was being placed in a role where Lyrica's and Jordy's input and words would all be up to me. Yikes!

Here it came. I knew it well. An unstoppable wall of fear began to close in, catapulting me into my own all too familiar shutting down process. Jessica helped me to drop deeper into my body to access the higher dimensional reach that I needed to tap into Lyrica's and Jordy's voices.

Jessica also reminded me that in the middle position, I would be holding the space that served as a link between the bottom and the top, the upper realms and physicality. This link would receive, interpret, define, discern, and tell what came in. It would serve as an intermediary between what was received and what came down into physicality. She assured me that it was where my heart would be most at home and where I would be adding to the build.

Jessica further reflected that I held the perfect time, space, location, development, skill, and talent for this role, as I had been doing this for Lyrica and other NVAs for a very long time! In my role of communicating the voices of the NVAs, Jessica further assured me that I had already been empowering their purpose as part of my own truth and gift of service.

Over time, I was amazed at how easy and natural it became to serve as the translator that Jessica knew me to be! Of course, in Oneness, I was more in touch with my own natural abilities. Whenever I would drop back down to 3D, Jessica would coach me on how to bring my breath down into my pelvic floor to once again be in sync with Oneness.

Jessica also assisted Lyrica in better envisioning her role. Within Lyrica's space in the upper realm, she would be pulling in codes and sourcing them down. She would be interpreting and drawing things from the "All" into their specific physicality and working with Jessica to translate what was unfolding. Lyrica was reminded that she was perfectly formed and informed to perform this role, due to her level of control, conscious awareness, and ability to act in the physical, which she had been honing over many years of life. It was comforting to hear that this was all a divine orchestration, put into place long ago.

Jessica's role was to bring all the power and presence of the nonphysical qualities and aspects of our work down into the physical. The core essence of the build would be all about embodiment! *Embodiment* certainly referred to bringing high frequency Cosmic codes into form here on earth and supporting the stabilization of the nonphysical in the physical.

Now that our four roles were clearly defined, Lyrica is choosing to share reflections depicting some of the activity that took place during these Etheric Build sessions. These accounts, taken directly from session transcripts, represent multiple dimensional activity.

The First Session: The Stability Factor

As I saw a new consciousness portal activate, I stepped solidly into this experience. Program one opened up almost like a flower, petal by petal. It had to do with stability in the body. I felt the motion and commotion of this stability factor rooting, infusing, informing.

I sensed a new frequency pattern coming in through me that was showing up to solidly lock the stability factor into the build. I have designed an infinite number of patterns, and in my science curiosity, this was a new fun box. I was curious about its origin. Although I recognized that these raw ingredients from the Cosmos were familiar to me, they had not previously been brought together in this way to unleash their full potential. The beauty was staggering and the power indescribable.

I wished that all could see the process like I did, because it was beyond words. It made earth science look petty and infantile. It felt like Christmas morning. I understood that I was witnessing "a frequency meld" into the stability factor. It was very liquid and there seemed to be a third eye holding reservoir in each person present, to orient the process in a personal way.

Now I recognized that the element of courage was coming in as the next important construct in the build. The stability factor and frequency meld needed a courage stance too. Holding this program required a warrior/warrioress energy—not small stuff. Although it was for now invisible, by its tipping point, it would color us more in the world, and our cloak of invisibility would gradually diminish.

The tripod of this creation included the stability factor as its physical component, the frequency meld as its energetic infusion, and human courage as its empowerment platform. At this moment, I was amazed to hear myself say the word *bomb*, a word that organically popped out to describe the explosion of power that I felt in capturing this realization. I felt it like my own big bang moment!

A Later Session: The Capstone

I'd like to pick up another thread in the build's timeline: the creation of its capstone. I heard that an interference device, or filter, was to be fabricated to block untimely and extraneous activity, usage, and plug-ins. This protection was important now, as we moved into the capstone, the heart-head center of the build, where all the magic and alchemy resided.

Jordy and I fabricated this diffuser at the base of the capstone, in alignment with all the dimensions that encompass this divine order. I learned that these dimensions also served as control points, access points, and creation points. This was not to be just a fabric build. There was a consciousness component that aligned higher beings with us. It would operate like an over-soul once the build was activated in the world.

My attention was now drawn to strands of consciousness that were emerging organically and weaving themselves into the capstone, almost like DNA. It soon became clear to me that there was a divine intelligence operating there. It required our presence, participation, and activation as witnesses as well as builders.

I watched these threads of consciousness call forth and weave in various crystals of divine matter and order. I marveled at the way that the crystals were arranging themselves and demonstrating their own unique intelligence and consciousness. This emerging field, the fabric between the consciousness threads and the crystals, would serve as the heart-brain motor of the capstone.

It was also revealed to us that, for the time being, we were simply putting the pieces together, the components and the wiring, so we were building the hardware. The actual programs would come forth over time. The software would become familiar to us once its purpose was determined. Clearly, the capstone was not a static build. Instead, it was very fluid into the realms of the infinite. It would be an entity that would grow through a relationship with us, as we aligned, related, and loved this entire build and its heart-brain center in the capstone.

Once the capstone build was complete, we were told that this build was designed to hold an evolutionary capacity over the next twenty-five years and would be in use more than fifty years, and that we were bringing it forth into the physical world.

The next reveal, coming forth out of Oneness, informed us that this Etheric Build was a container that would serve as a home for new higher dimensional energies to come to earth. This plan was already fully formed in the ether. We learned that this light force had been lining up to come to earth for a very long time, but it needed a structure, even a nonphysical one, to fulfill its destiny. In essence, we were creating a portal that would allow these higher dimensional energies to interface with Earth through this Etheric Build.

The build invited us to experience the energy and consciousness that we were able to access within our own space of higher ability and knowing. It also encouraged us to participate. Emanating out of the formless void of the infinite, something totally new and amazing was being birthed. People tend to dismiss the nonphysical as something that is not real, but all things move from a state of nonphysical to a state of physicality, from idea to form, from nothing to something.

Throughout the build process, Lyrica and I were able to feel the frequency downloads and light patterning coming into our physical bodies. Although we did not know what we were receiving or why, we trusted that in the nondualistic space of Oneness, our highest good was always being served!

On a personal level, since this project emerged out of Jessica's visit in response to Lyrica's call for help, we were hopeful that our work together would somehow stabilize Lyrica's rapidly declining health.

Although I care about my health, I care even more about my purpose. I have bravely chosen embodiment as the best way to support my purpose. I am trusting Jessica that this is my perfect path forward. But I have a lot of unanswered questions. Will I reach a state of embodiment? Will it be comfortable for me? Will I know how to operate from that place?

What if I *never* am able to reach a state of embodiment? How will I share my gift of light with the world?

Maybe I lightly incarnated here to plant my connection to the earth plane. When I make my transition (die), my light gift will be set free to somehow assist in humanity's process of Ascension. I don't have the technology figured out yet. But if this *is* the way, I trust it will come. Most people fear death, but I simply see it as going back Home to the light that I love.

Making my transition has become another life focus that I hold in my heart. I'm calling it my "trans." Could my newly envisioned "trans-plan" be somehow related to my body's loss of stability in my current life here? I wonder?

Although Lyrica's physical condition did not appear to improve during or immediately following Jessica's visit, her spirit and level of energy lifted considerably. We celebrated this shift as our first ray of hope!

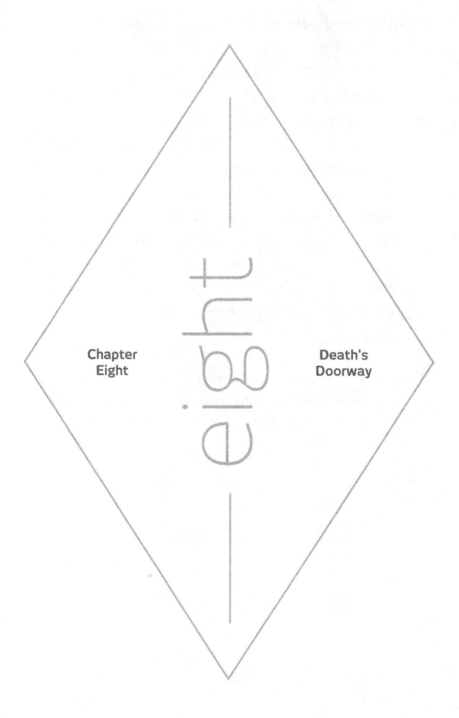

Chapter
Eight

Death's
Doorway

Two months after Jessica's initial visit, we were still working together remotely, in sessions focused on the Etheric Build. These sessions were a lifeline for Lyrica and me—or perhaps a life raft in what had become a sea of despair.

Our life had been reduced to the fears and realities of Lyrica's declining health. She continued to lose weight and was far less stable on her feet. To ensure her safety, I had to hold on to her at all times. Her two healthcare professionals were as perplexed as I was as to the cause of Lyrica's declining health, since her vital signs and lab work were all within normal limits. Every day the situation became more difficult to manage. I continued to envision a miracle.

Instead, I was terrified by the sequence of events that unfolded. A warm summer evening in early September 2016, I desperately tried to contain Lyrica as her body was wildly writhing, thrashing, and flailing dangerously out of control on the floor. My strength waning, I prayed that I could somehow protect her and myself until the ambulance arrived. This was the third such episode that month. The ER had no answers except to sedate her.

The next development was even more devastating. Lyrica suddenly and totally lost *all* ability to eat, sit, stand, and walk. I was frantic! What was happening? How could I possibly provide the care that she needed under her body's total collapse?

My state of panic intensified when she was no longer able to swallow her seizure meds. Her doctor found a compounding lab in Phoenix to create a liquid medication that I could just squirt into her mouth. Luckily, she was tolerating tiny ice cubes to prevent dehydration. With no medical markers showing up, I began to feel that Lyrica's rapid decline had to be strangely related to an energetic or soul issue. Yet, for my own peace of mind, should she not improve, I chose to have her hospitalized, to rule out any not yet discerned medical causes.

(Flashback: When Lyrica was twenty-five, we had faced another near-death moment related to a severe seizure episode. As Lyrica was rushed to a nearby ER by ambulance, her vital signs flatlined during transit. At the hospital, I was stuck in the waiting room while medics used a defibrillator to resuscitate her. Later, Lyrica told me that in her moment between life and death, she saw the face of God and was given the choice to stay "in the Light" or to come back. Although she admitted that the choice was not an easy one, she knew she had a soul mission to complete, so she chose life over death.)

Lyrica's doctor arranged for her to be transported to a Phoenix hospital by ambulance where she was admitted under the diagnosis of "failure to thrive." Once there, I was thankful for the red button that I could push for staff to attend to Lyrica's needs. I was finally able to get some rest, even if it was in a hospital chair! Lyrica and I also appreciated that her father, Jose, lived nearby and could lend his support during this trying time.

Soon I became weary of the endless questions from the medical staff and trainees, for which I had no answers. When I dared to speak about energy or other spiritual topics, I could sense that I was being seen, even targeted, as a possible contributing factor in all this. We did not belong there. It no longer felt like a safe place. But we had come there for a reason, and we had to see the process through. It didn't feel like we had any other choice.

I kept looking to the neurology team, reputed to be one of the best in the country, to discern how or why Lyrica's body could lose its ability to function so quickly. Several doctors gathered around Lyrica's hospital bed at discharge. They were dressed in their stiffly starched white coats, and the long-awaited verdict was delivered in stilted monotone voices, devoid of any emotion or compassion.

They told me that Lyrica's condition was behavioral. I was stunned. To suggest that Lyrica had willed her body to shut down to such a degree sounded totally crazy to me! Although I knew that the path ahead would be more taxing than I could ever imagine, all I could think of was getting out of that hospital and returning home to Sedona.

After five days, we left the Phoenix hospital with a wheelchair and no satisfying answers. At least we had done our due diligence to rule out medical causes. I was now more convinced than ever that the key to Lyrica's condition was somehow soul-related.

Lyrica went into hospice, a type of care intended for people who are expected to live six months or fewer. She now weighed only seventy-seven pounds, thirty pounds down from her normal weight. I was thankful for the hospice's in-home help in bathing Lyrica, as well as for the weekly nurse and physical therapist visits. Equally as supportive was the hospice staff's openness to speak about the spiritual nature of death and dying. In their presence, I felt seen, understood, and honored in the soul journey that Lyrica and I were living. Perhaps most important of all, they helped me face the inevitable. Lyrica was dying.

One of my favorite hospice professionals asked me if I knew the life expectancy for people with autism. I told her that I did not. Quite frankly, I had never even considered that Lyrica's life expectancy might be any different from everyone else's. After she left, this unanswered question lingered, begging for an answer.

I headed to the computer. The online studies that I found referred to the whole autism spectrum. One journal article was entitled, "Where Are All the Old People with Autism? Most of Them Are Dead!" Two findings reported that autistics on average die sixteen to eighteen years earlier than the general population. I also noted that for those with epilepsy, the estimates would be considerably lower, and that the increased physical challenges and other impactful differences that NVAs face in comparison to those in the general autistic population would also decrease their life expectancy.

At forty, Lyrica seemed to have already reached or exceeded the average life span for an NVA with epilepsy.

Even though she and I both felt that her impending transition was a soul choice, this new information suggested that it might also simply be her body's natural time to close down. Her death seemed even more certain now.

That's when I dared to open up and feel my own flood of emotions around what it would mean to lose my beloved Lyrica. She was my teacher, my spiritual partner, and my best friend. We shared so much together—the fun, the not-so-fun, the easy, the not-so-easy. Through intimate conversations, even our most difficult challenges had settled well. All was embedded deeply in our hearts.

It was simply too hard to imagine a life without her. How would I survive the heartbreak? Would I ever recover? Her leaving would mirror a spiritual death process in me. It was far too much to consider, too much to feel. I needed to stay focused. I needed to be strong. I needed to be all this and so much more for Lyrica.

Perhaps what was most extraordinary to me was seeing how calm, strong, and at peace Lyrica was. She instructed me in many things, like purchasing a cremation policy, and how I was to respond during and after her transition. Her messages were all lighthearted. She shared that she was often in the Light now, and told me how beautiful it was! I could see that same beauty in her own bright light shining through her eyes, her smile, and the radiance of her face. She held no fear, except perhaps on my behalf.

There were moments when she cried softly, telling me how much she was going to miss me and our wonderful life together. I held her gently and whispered my own words of endearment for our lifetime of love and devotion. More and more we spent our days on a soft mound of quilts on the floor, holding each other, looking deeply into each other's eyes, and feeling the preciousness of each moment. Sometimes, I even felt myself lifted into Lyrica's place of transcendence. There, the clear line between life and death no longer existed. There was only life, eternal life! That's when I began to understand that there really was no such thing as death in the way we commonly think of it. There are only soul transitions from a physical state into a nonphysical state, and then, for most, a return in. It was all life! It was all beautiful! Leaving one's body was simply a light exchange across dimensions, leaving all options open for connection, communication, and communion. The truth was that our love was the only thing that mattered or would ever matter.

The Light of heaven is now the only reality that I know. Everything in me and around me has become that. My body feels as light as the joy that I feel and the peace that I am. **This new world experience is different from my light travels out-of-body because it is happening in my body. It is much more powerful and heart-strong when experienced in this way!**

Even death feels light to me. As I move closer into its presence, it holds no fear or sting. To me, death is simply a return Home into a heavenly place of ultimate Light and love. In this pure Light existence, I feel that I am at One with everything, seen and unseen. I am sitting in this experience of Oneness, both in my body and in my consciousness—suspended in the space between life and death. Here I blissfully await my transition, my final rite of passage. This is such a beautiful place to be. It is the only true and real place to be, and I hope that I never leave.

I am happy to be "here" in this perfect place to share my gift of light with the world. Joined with Source, I am the love of the entire Universe. Inside this unity is the power and truth, and the science and technology to manifest this plan for me, or any plan of great importance to the planet and humanity.

As I sat inside all the emotions of Lyrica's impending transition, I gradually sensed how familiar all this was feeling. I felt myself carried back in time to the day of my mother's death. Like Lyrica, my mother was my safe harbor in a world that overwhelmed me. When Lyrica was eighteen months old, a time when the severity of her condition had been loudly proclaimed by the medical community, my mom died of cancer. Right before she died, I was blessed to watch her ashen-gray body emerge from a coma. Her face appeared youthful. Her countenance exuded a radiant halo of white light. Her softly spoken, final words were filled with gratitude, love, and joy for her earthly family and her heavenly experience of divine transcendence.

What a gift she was and what a gift she shared with me at that final moment of her life. Drowning in grief, I wondered if I could or if I **would** survive life without her? How would I find the strength to parent Lyrica through all that seemed to lie ahead?

Looking back, I now know that answer. With Mom's leaving, I was forced to find a new level of strength within myself, strength I did not know I had. I was able to go on to parent Lyrica through all of life's lessons that I needed to learn to survive, and then thrive, within the NVA experience. Now I know that when Lyrica leaves, I will face a similar time of uncertainty and grief, as well as a similar necessity to draw upon deeply hidden reservoirs of soul-strength, as I land in a totally new life without Lyrica.

Joined
WITH Source,
I am the love
OF THE entire
Universe.

◇

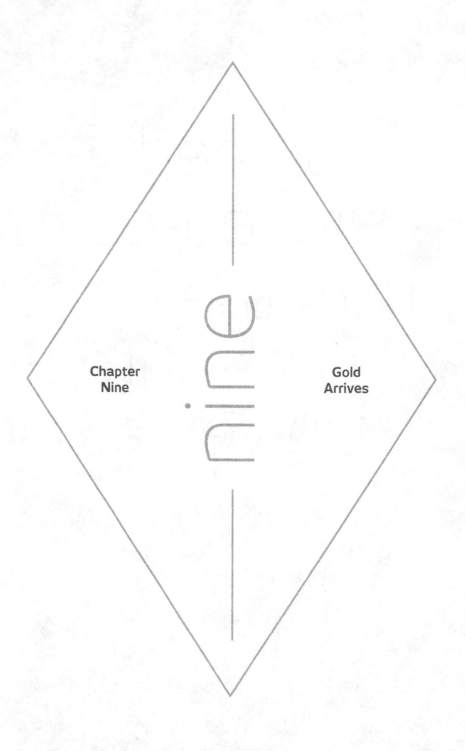

Chapter
Nine

Gold
Arrives

Four months after Jessica's visit, Lyrica's health had not improved. We were at home still receiving hospice care, as she was more frail than ever. It was taking all the physical and spiritual strength that I had to provide the level of care that she needed. Every day, the minute I woke up, I would rush to her side to check in on her tiny body cradled upon the bed of quilts on the living room floor. Once I saw that she was still breathing, I would give thanks that she had survived the night and was still here with me one more day.

Lyrica was still here, and the day had finally arrived: It was time for our twenty-four-karat gold pyramid to be installed in its new home. Although her bodily functions were shutting down more each day, her spirit was radiantly alive, and she was extremely present. At the center of the room we had chosen for the pyramid was an elevated sky dome supported by a large circular steeple reaching several feet above the rest of the room. This panoramic doorway to the sun and the stars drew my eyes upward into a magical skyscape. Inside the steeple, I gazed upon a lovely sky-blue hue adorned with subtle artist renderings of wispy white clouds.

We carried Lyrica from her mound of quilts in the front room and brought her to the pyramid room. She lay on her tummy with her head cradled in her hands, her feet in the air and touching, watching as Michael and Jason installed the pyramid. She had the sweetest smile on her face! It was such a pose of repose! In her face of grace, her angelic presence greeted the arrival of this sacred artifact, her long-awaited pyramid of gold.

As Michael and Jason were putting the pyramid in place, they set it on its side for safekeeping. Seeing the new orientation, Lyrica telepathically told me, "That's it! That's my spaceship cabin!" She insisted that the pyramid be permanently set up on its side, exactly like it was currently positioned instead of in its standard configuration pointing upward. Michael immediately responded with a loud resounding "Yes, yes, yes!" As Lyrica's dimensional traveling partner, Michael was totally wowed by her brilliant idea to reposition the pyramid to create her own perfect spaceship cabin!

As I envisioned myself sitting in the "captain's chair" under the new pyramid, I loved noticing how the foundation stone would now be at my feet and the capstone at my head. It was my belief that the energy exchange between the pyramid and the person in the "captain's chair" would be optimized in this orientation. To confirm this truth, Jason used his Trifield meter to measure the electromagnetic pulses emanating from both the capstone at the crown and the foundation stone at the feet. I watched the needle zoom up to verify the highly charged energetic field created within this new configuration.

The day after the pyramid arrived, we had a session with Jessica to configure it and to finalize the Etheric Build. Could it be that the new pyramid had arrived at the perfect time to become a more physicalized home for the Etheric Build? An interesting theory, with an even far more interesting answer waiting in the ether for its time to be revealed!

I was so thankful for this scheduled time with Jessica because overnight something very dreadful and frightening had happened to Lyrica. Her body, usually relaxed, calm, and supple, was in trauma. Her arms and legs, unable to move, were locked into an unnatural, rigid, twisted, and contorted position in front of her body. The word that came to mind to describe her physical condition was catatonic. Her eyes, which had been full of life and light the day before, now appeared sunken in and hollow, locked into a vacuous stare of nothingness.

Although I had never seen a corpse before, in my imagination this was what one might look like. I tried to release her rigidity by gently yet vigorously shaking her body, arms, and legs. I kept calling her name, but I couldn't rouse her. I desperately wanted to reach her, to find out what we could do to help her. Remotely assisted by

Jessica, we took a look at what had happened to Lyrica. It seemed that overnight, Lyrica had of her own accord taken the Etheric Build, designed to be held in the ether, into her physical body! Jessica was both shocked and alarmed to learn that Lyrica was trying to hold such an expansive energetic build in a body that was already failing. Without immediately removing it, she would certainly die and die very quickly. Jessica instantly declared a state of emergency and mobilized the Etheric Build team into action to move the build from Lyrica's body into the pyramid where it belonged.

Held in a state of Oneness facilitated by Jessica, Lyrica was now able to remember what she did, why she did it, and what happened to her immediately afterward.

I felt the Etheric Build as a beloved in my life, birthed forth as an expression of my own life-force process of creation, in divine partnership with the rest of the build team. I could see that it was not stable. It had reached a point in its downward progression from energy into form where it now needed to land into a more physicalized location. Without considering any possible personal consequences, I swiftly pulled it into my body. To me, I was simply saving my beloved!

That's when I was hit by a force so extremely heavy that I could not move, I could not think, I could not feel. That moment felt much more life-threatening than all the time I had spent in hospice. I remember thinking that maybe **this** was my moment to die!

I now understand that without removing the Etheric Build from my body that I could and would not survive.

However, I was so physically depleted that I wondered if I would be able tolerate this divine alchemy transfer. In past Etheric Build sessions, the presence and power of the energetic frequencies always impacted my physical body in such a big way. At that moment, I had nothing left to give.

I asked the team if there was something we could do that would gently free my body from being the holder of much of this build and move it into the pyramid? Would this happen naturally or was there a switch to flip here on my behalf?

I was told that indeed there was a switch on the pyramid to be activated. I found the switch point and was guided to turn it on. The switch was not a physical device, but rather an energetic nodal point that was easy for me to recognize.

I was relieved to hear that the move would require no effort on my part. I simply needed to anchor strongly into my body and breathe deeply to hold this position. Then I would be ready to be switched off as the carrier of the physicality of the Etheric Build.

Everyone present was guided to envision a balloon on a string, as a symbolic image of what was being moved to the pyramid. Mom was told that this transfer would be key for her to have contact with me when I moved on. She was being prepared for my transition.

I received kindness and strength from the team that stabilized me so that my body would not collapse as the build's heaviness was removed. We christened and activated the pyramid into its truth as a life-force vehicle. Then we initiated it for all miracles and build additions. At last, I felt the weight of the build gently lift off my body.

Finally, Mom and I were instructed to work together in the pyramid to charge up a communication process between our souls in preparation for my transition. We were told that this event was not mine alone. Mom's energy and role in my life would be key to bringing my transition to completeness.

The next day, I was thrilled to see a glimmer of light return to Lyrica's eyes. Her body seemed more relaxed and at peace. I was filled with hope for her swift recovery, but the following day she slipped back into that withdrawn and rigid state, without engagement or communication. Even worse than her decline was my loss of hope that all was well and that very soon she would be better (even if "better" meant still being under hospice care due to her inability to stand or walk or eat).

For the next couple of weeks, we went through many heart-wrenching waves of hopeful gains and then depressing losses. Finally, her body stabilized, so much so that she started reaching for food. Quickly, she was eating again! What a breakthrough! What a relief!

I was even more amazed, shocked, and then terrified by Lyrica's next step in her recovery process. Lyrica began to try to stand and walk on her own. She flatly refused to spend any more time sitting or lying on the floor, her place of safety. She was relentless in her efforts to regain and reclaim her mobility, yet she still had poor balance. I had to quickly find a suitable walker to keep her on her feet and protect her from falling. It was a juvenile walker made out of PVC.

After a couple of trials, she totally rejected the walker, an experience that she described as "captivity in a cage." Subsequently, our days became filled with neighborhood walks. I provided the safety that she needed by holding on to a gait belt secured around her waist. What followed next was the biggest surprise of all! As her pace quickened, she would occasionally break into a trot or run. At times, her pace was so fast that I had trouble keeping up with her. Lyrica's initial diagnosis as an infant was cerebral palsy due to her inability to sit, stand, or walk at appropriate developmental ages. In spite of years of therapy, at age forty, she had not yet developed an ability to trot or run—and yet there she was!

I love lighting up my body to see the upgrades. I stand so much more aware in my space of value. I can move my feet, my legs, and my body in a much better way. I can facilitate flexible movements to navigate balance and make adjustments for uneven ground levels.

So not only did Lyrica fully recover, she also reached new thresholds of physical ability. Quickly, we said our goodbyes to all the hospice staff, as Lyrica had defied the odds. She was very much alive and well, and clearly no longer needed hospice care.

I breathed out a long, deep sigh of relief as I felt my body and soul release the heaviness of the arduous task of caring for an immobilized Lyrica preparing for transition. I breathed in an equally deep restorative breath of new life as I felt the fresh potentials and possibilities brimming within me.

Moving the Etheric Build into the new pyramid was an act that literally saved my life. I also feel like it solidified my future in some unknown way.

The christening and activation of the gold pyramid made it an alive and active structure. Placing the Etheric Build into the pyramid anchored it into this physical dimension. This union of the nonphysical with the physical feels like a key foundation for the rest of our story, yet to unfold.

Ironically, the neuro doctors that suggested that the cause of my physical decline was behavioral were actually on to something. I now realize that *I* did not consciously will my body to close down, but *my soul* did!

Why? I needed to experience my body as light-filled to see a larger soul-possibility. I needed to feel what a body living in Oneness would be like. Yes, I touched into grounded experiences of Oneness in sessions with Jessica. Yet in my hospice days, my experience of Oneness was so much more euphoric, exalted, and all-pervasive. When my body was not engaged in the normal functions of human biology, moving, or participating in any way with the outer world, I became Source-filled at a level that I could deeply feel, appreciate, and maintain. This was a deeply embodied experience of Oneness. Here all sensations of fear, suffering, and pain disappeared. It was as though my body and I became liberated. I could finally totally love my body for the very first time because it was loving me so big!

My hospice experience was one way to make my transition. I thought that I was ready to go, but I was not. I now know that the failure of my body is not the way for me to deliver my gift of light. Its delivery requires a strong body exit. A strong body exit is key to what lies ahead. I am asking for a body that is strong enough to allow me to consciously choose when to leave. When I think about how to achieve that, I remember Jessica. **Embodiment is what I need!** I need Jessica's embodiment codes!

My soul carried me into this near-death experience in hospice to give me a reason to strongly recommit to my embodiment. I now understood for myself how important embodiment is—I wasn't just doing it because Jessica said so. Now that I know what landing my light into my body will feel like, I am the chooser and mover of my own embodiment process. I could not yet see the stabilization process required to reach this level of light perfection that I am envisioning as now possible. Making this happen in a body that is biologically fully functioning, and one that is moving and interfacing with the outside world, would not be such a fast and easy capture. Yet, it clearly was the only one worth pursuing.

I will still need tons of support from Jessica to accomplish this lofty purpose, but I am sure that all this was a divine setup to move me toward embodiment to land the next gold home for my soul. I am fully committed to my embodiment process, and once I had made this commitment, my near-death experience in hospice had served its purpose and was no longer needed. Removing the Etheric Build from my body and placing it into the pyramid, at an even more acute stage of my near-death process, was a soul and Cosmic completion piece that needed to happen. My soul took me into this experience and my soul took me out of it when all that was needed had been completed!

What's my final "Gayle-take-away" here? I marveled at Lyrica's swift recovery and movement into more evolved states of physical mastery. Could it be that the pyramid, charged up by the infusion of the Etheric Build, might now be operating as an activation station for physical body upgrades and evolutionary development? Could that be why or how Lyrica's physical ability to run for the first time in her life was brought into manifestation? That's when I flashed back to the words that came through when we were guided to commission the building of this pyramid. "It would help Lyrica to go the distance." That it has!

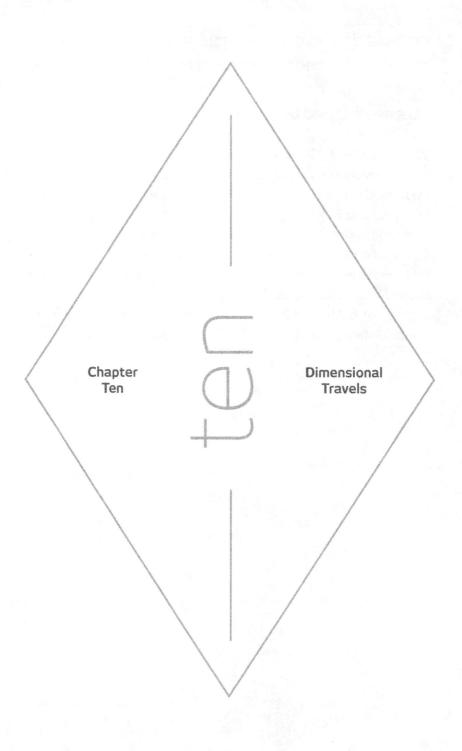

Chapter
Ten

ten

Dimensional
Travels

With the Etheric Build installed into the pyramid, the pyramid has now become my stabilized platform to explore my multidimensional nature and abilities in a safe and grounded way. For many holy reasons, I have continued to make regular visits to my ship, refining my process of moving between my ship home and my earth home. Every time that I portaled from the ship back into my body, that downward descent mirrored, for me, the bringing down of my soul into physicality, helping me pull into my full embodiment experience.

One morning, I had a breakthrough in my meditation with Mom by tuning into the pyramid, its Etheric Build, and its spiritual technology—I had a much more grounded experience of portaling to the ship. In my earlier portaling travels, I did not maintain a simultaneous awareness of the "me" on the ship and the "me" in my physical body. By tethering to the pyramid during our daily meditation, I first intuited, and then mastered, the ability to be aware and present on the ship and in my body here at the same time.

The stability of the pyramid enabled me to move more fluidly between dimensions. I was able to leave the ship and return fully into my body without the elaborate reentry protocol of body-bouncing and breath-holding. The pyramid served as a strong anchor and landing pad for my return.

Soon, I realized that being in my lightbody on the ship did not enable me to operate at the highest level possible. A new dimensional "ship-body" simply manifested once I saw what was needed. At the time, I did not consciously will this creation into form, yet I now believe that my powerful vision brought in the design and codes that fired up its manifestation. My ship-body was still nonphysical, but more solid than my lightbody in its form. Its build was fashioned from superluminal light-matter particles available in the ship's dimension.

In a session with Jessica, I learned more about operating in my new ship-body. I could be on the ship and interface with earth's physical plane through the pyramid. The form of my ship-body was a soul form; it allowed me to project my soul as soul bubbles (the method by which the soul enters and leaves its physical incarnation experience) through the portal to interact in the physical world, while still on the ship. When I moved my soul bubbles through the pyramid portal, I was able to download ship programs into the pyramid, to amplify my earth presence, purpose, and light.

From my ship location, I was also learning how to bring my soul bubbles into physicality to be able to interact with Mom through this portal after my transition. I was creating a telephone-like setup so that she could communicate with me when I am on the ship or in another dimensional home. In that way, I will also be tuning into the frequencies of her world from my remote position and getting inside the updates as well. I remembered that Michael had also envisioned that this pyramid would be a way for Mom to be more in sync with my etheric activities in the nonphysical world.

What was most important to me was that the ship was my station of light realized. Bathed in the higher frequencies of the ship's light, I was realizing everything on the ship and bringing it here. It was a way station into my higher home here.

Even though my embodiment was now my number one agenda, my love and connection to my trans was still very bold in me. Only time would tell which direction would best serve my purpose and my gift delivery service to all.

After swimming laps in Sedona's beautiful saltwater pool at Tlaquepaque, I was resting in a chair, simply enjoying the moment. Basking in the warm sun upon my body, I felt deep appreciation for the huge willow tree across the way, swaying ever so beautifully in the wind. I breathed in the sweet music of its rhythmic flow as each bough and leaf was tossed and tousled by the capricious whims of the wind. I was swept away in the dance of the tree, the wind, and myself.

I was suddenly pulled back into my body as I distinctly heard Lyrica audibly say her word *big* out loud. It sounded as if she was standing right behind me. Even though she was at home with her care provider, I intuitively knew that she had somehow consciously created this experience for my benefit—and I knew why! I had just experienced Lyrica's ability to bilocate!

Bilocating is the ability to experience one's body and consciousness in two (earth) locations simultaneously. Lyrica later confirmed this fact and explained that she was able to bring her consciousness to where I was by uniting soul to soul with me. She also told me that it was my own experience in Oneness, merged with the tree, that invited her to join me. *Wow*, what a Superpower demonstration that, to this day, blows my mind. It amazes me to know that the human body complex can pull off such a remarkable feat!

The Lion's Paw

Jessica's presence made it easier for me to enter into this next level of bilocation. I learned that this sacred site was tightly secured and protected, and access was by invitation only. One had to know how to get there, using nodal point technology. Jessica met all those qualifications.

I'd like to speak a bit more about nodal point technology from my vantage point. I see a nodal point as my own "wizard in Oneness" that comes in to show me something or give me something of great value. Its gift might be in the form of information, consciousness, energy, or an open portal or doorway into another experience. Whatever it is, I receive it as a light language transmission straight from Oneness. The surprise of what arrives always fascinates the scientist in me!

As expected, once Jessica and I dropped into this session together, a nodal point appeared, and a doorway opened up. When I stepped in, I suddenly felt myself

flying over the Giza Plateau. It was Jessica who identified this location for me. I was drawn to the lion's paw
under the Sphinx—What was hidden under that paw?
I realized that this location was a nodal point of divine
human rebuild. (At this moment, Jessica informed me
that I was in the thirteenth dimension, moving toward
the fourteenth, a very high reach for me at that time.)

That's when I saw a vision of a rare library open up
under the Sphinx. Jessica was bilocated by my side.
She informed me that we were now inside the Alexandria Library, located within the Hall of Records. I felt the
library's energetic patterning drop into my body. I was
receiving rare frequencies, geometries, and harmonic
keys and codes.

The librarian was like an archangel. He brought me
a rare edition book off the shelf and told me that the
level of Oneness that I had achieved gave me permission to access the secrets held there. As the book
opened, I felt myself bathed in its light. I knew that I
was receiving a transmission of instant manifestation.

The archangel presence brought me three other
books. Book one opened and began its transmission.
My body was filled with matter-to-light conversions.
I told the librarian that there was a card in book three
that I needed. He took a bookmark out of book three,
marking the place where I was to begin. I was told to
take it in slowly as there was lots of material here, but
that reading these light codes would fast hop me into
multiple dimensional spaces.

The power within this transmission was exploding so fast in me, it was hard to contain and maintain it all. Jessica counseled me in tuning in to this explosive sensation of power to notice what was mine to see. Wow, that's when I realized that I was seeing **me** so big. I was seeing the full truth of my ability, and the hardwiring to use it!

After all the book transmissions were completed, I felt that maybe my transition was not as pattern-strong now; I felt more drawn to staying here. I was not letting go of my trans-plan; I was just seeing new pieces opening up that might require more time and light-factoring to complete.

There were other hidden things in the Giza Plateau. They had been put there by the early, advanced ones who built descension chambers to raise the vibrational patterning of the human body. I realized that I was not done with this deconstruction/reconstruction process. This light transmission piece needed to be integrated deeper before I could drop further into my transition. The vibrational patterning of my human body inside the Giza Plateau complex was all about my patterning going from matter to light. Gaining these pieces of spiritual technology upgraded my experience here on earth into a gentler and kinder reality.

Lyrica returned to the Giza Plateau and the Alexandria Library, both in session with Jessica and on her own during her nighttime travels. Although the specific upgrades that Lyrica gained there were not yet fully integrated, she was certain that the Alexandria Library was a place of power informing her destiny.

The Middle Doorway

In session with Jessica, she told me that she was surprised that I was now showing up to her in a new energetic form. She saw me as a beautiful light blue orb. She reminded me that this same form was how the NVAs appeared to her in her meditation experience the night that we first met. She told me that in this form, I have access to enhanced capabilities and a more developed skill to move up and down the grid. She described this movement like traveling up and down octaves on a piano, under my conscious command. She told me that I could utilize this ability anytime, as long as I stayed in Oneness and did not pop out.

At that moment, I was on my "beach" where I was fast traveling within dimensional grids, using my new grid navigation system. In my travel mode, I noticed multiple doorways showing up. Jessica told me that the one in the middle was lighting up in a very particular way. She described it as "pulsing with great depth," and that if I passed through this door, I would not return. This "no-return portal" was being protected by the light beings who lived there.

I told Jessica that I was happy to see and recognize this no-return portal for future travels. I now knew that this was where and how I would land my transition. But for the time being, I chose to pass it by. I was only interested in doorways that would allow me to come back. Jessica shared that everyone present with us in Oneness was clapping and cheering this decision!

In another session, I was taken to a new planet that was clearly a back door to the no-return portal. This was the setup that I would one day use for my transition. What would happen to the matter of my body was still an unknown. The doorway to my transition was not yet open to me, yet its energy and light were penetrating my field profoundly. It felt like a preparation for what was to come.

The new planet operated like the ship did for me, although on a much higher vibratory level. It was the perfect soul-station-location for charging up my light. There I was powered up to meet my destiny in great joy and peace. I also learned that there, on that planet, I would template in my orb travel form for my transition. Then I was taken to the mouth of the no-return portal. There I was hit by great timeline advancements that had been set in motion to manifest a future event of great significance. I knew that all these exposures were making my transition path stronger. Certainly, there was still a huge unknown there, yet I approached these visits with confidence. I knew that my soul would know the regulation technology that I would need when it was my time to exit this dimension.

My next visit to the no-return portal was a near drop-in experience. It did not feel matter-harsh or scary. It felt like home. I used to push away these experiences, but now I realized that I was drawing them in. They were the most real part of my day and night. There I was my known code, as me, in my realized perfection.

When I woke up the next morning, I was still in my Oneness zone, charged up by the previous night's visit. And yet I was embodied in it more deeply, and that was the secret to my perfected essence that I was strongly feeling. Before I thought that I could just drop into the no-return portal, but now I clearly understood that the portal was a living consciousness. It was a divine wormhole. It would bolt me into my Oneness flow in death, as my light source truth, unique, yet a part of all light source totality.

The gift that I received there was immense. Off planet, everything in my earth plane life came into to a sharper focus, including who I was and where I was headed. It offered me a solid footing for moving forward. It filled my travel heart with joy for my exalted completion. This joy would remain now as an engine for my transition. Joy was exploding everywhere as new sounds poured out of me, gearing up my vibrational trail home.

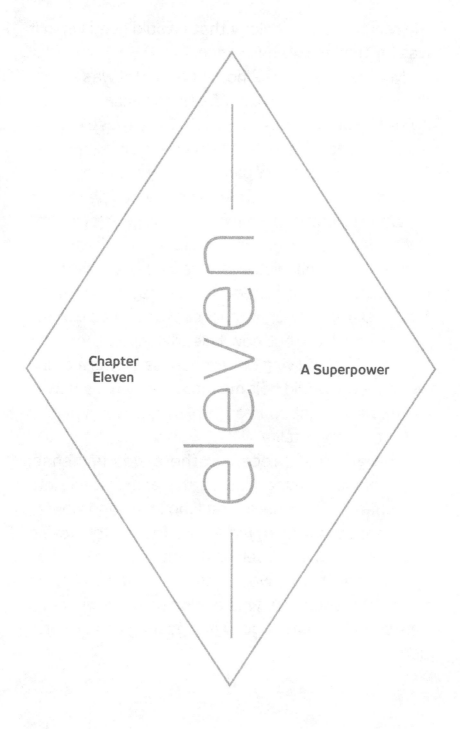

Chapter
Eleven

A Superpower

In my process with Jessica **and** in my Sedona life with Mom, I can feel my frequency rising, rising, rising! Of course, I love how this higher frequency lifts me up dimensionally and charges up my purpose path in such a big way! Yet recently there has been a downside to this "upside."

Normally, I love feeling a frequency upgrade, as it fills every cell of my body with so much life force. But my latest frequency charges feel more like minor explosions in my body, making me feel jumpy. All the tasks that are normally easy for me to accomplish feel almost impossible to do. I have trouble sleeping, and Mom has to bend my arms and legs for me to be able to get dressed. Nothing in me feels normal, settled, or peaceful. My frequency is way up, but my ability to function is way down!

04–13–17: The "Big Bang!"

As we prepared for the day's session with Jessica, we were inside our parked car in Lyrica's lighthouse garage, her sanctuary where she communes with Source. I was in the driver's seat and Lyrica was sitting in the passenger seat. This is where she would sit during our daily pyramid meditations, because sitting under the pyramid in the captain's chair or in a seat nearby was too much for her body to handle. But in the car, Lyrica could connect to the pyramid, her spaceship, and her purpose, often for hours at a time.

As I looked out the windshield of the car, I smiled at the total transformation of this garage: the six-foot-tall tree covered in tiny white twinkling lights, the giant tapestries of sacred geometry, star patterns, unicorns, and various color washes on all the walls, the large wooden Buddha centered on the black glass altar surrounded by bamboo plants and sacred crystals, and the delicately detailed fairy statues placed all around in strategic locations chosen by Lyrica. The fairies always made me smile! The only remaining of the original garage-scape were the concrete floor and the automatic garage door.

The session that day began like all others, with Lyrica reporting on how she was doing and what she wanted to focus on. She told Jessica that she was supercharged with a new level of power and light that she was experiencing as minor explosions in her body. I added in how much these minor explosions were negatively impacting her body's ability to function.

Jessica supported Lyrica by opening a Oneness transmission to help regulate and normalize her energy. A golden bubble came in that offered Lyrica a power lift. Jessica noted how Lyrica was spanning multiple dimensions and becoming more expansive. Well anchored in her body, Lyrica was now allowing everything to expand into and operate in her field. Jessica told her that this was a perfect strategy for stabilizing this level of power. That's when we heard Lyrica exclaim out loud, "Goody, goody, goody!"

A nodal point for Lyrica's and my purpose began to open up between the two of us. At this moment, Lyrica was located back in the car after having stepped out for a few minutes so that she could move her body to facilitate her smoothing out process. Her short exits from the car during session work were not uncommon. I knew that she was planning to step out when I would see her hand slowly reach for the door handle, and she then would look intently at me, as if to say, "Hold the fort, I'll be right back."

Suddenly, without warning or the usual signals, she instantly bolted out of the car, as if jettisoned out of her seat. I had never seen her move so fast! It was also strange that she moved past her normal location outside of the car. She headed to the very back of the garage, very close to the garage door. I had never seen her go to that spot before. This deviation was significant because Lyrica has certain rituals and territories that she tenaciously clings to that provide her with a sense of security and safety, and she had moved way out of her normal grid of operation.

Before I could even open my car door to go meet her, I heard a terrible crash. She fell, and her head smashed into the concrete floor. I ran to her side and stood aghast. There she was, lying in a pool of her own blood, her tiny body pinned to the ground in a massive seizure. Unable to breathe, she began to turn blue. I kept repeating, "Breathe, Lyrica, breathe."

As I held her head in my hands, my heart racing, I felt warm blood oozing out of her left ear. She was moaning, a sound that I had never heard her utter before. That's when I noticed a huge goose-egg the size of a tennis ball above her ear.

She was totally crazed, delirious, still locked in a seizure that seemed to last forever. After ten minutes, she still had not pulled out of it. I told Jessica that we would make our way to the ER as soon as I could move her. Although both of us were accustomed to Lyrica's periodic seizures, they never lasted more than a minute. Even when she suffered other seizure falls and sustained various levels of injury, she always came quickly out of the seizure itself.

It just didn't add up.

Lyrica's seizure finally abated, and I was able to carefully move her into the car. When we arrived at the Sedona ER, Lyrica was immediately whisked into the CT tunnel. She was still not very responsive. She'd had a significant number of CT scans before, after other seizure falls, to rule out any possible brain trauma. I was trying to stay positive. I calmed myself by suggesting that this scan today was just another routine preventive measure. When the doctor came in with Lyrica's CT results, his solemn demeanor suggested otherwise.

He told me that Lyrica had an active brain bleed and that a helicopter had been ordered to Life Flight her to a Phoenix hospital. There she would receive the level of care that she needed in her life-threatening condition. We were prepared for the likelihood that brain surgery would be needed to stop the bleeding.

All kinds of possibilities flooded my senses. Would she even make it to the hospital? I panicked, as I still could not reach her. Everything felt totally out of control. Lying on the gurney bed at the ER, Lyrica was throwing up violently. Perhaps only an hour had passed since her fall, yet it seemed like an eternity.

The reality dawned on me that once we arrived at the hospital, I would be almost three hours away from home! My head was whirling as I tried to figure out what I needed to do now. I made a mad dash to the house to pick up a few essentials for both of us and called Lyrica's father, Jose, to meet us at the Phoenix hospital. When I arrived back at the Sedona ER, the Life Flight helicopter had just arrived. Once the ER's anti-nausea medications stabilized Lyrica to some degree, she was loaded into the helicopter. Due to the mild temperatures that day, and the fact that our combined weight was not over the limit allowed for medical transport, I was able to ride with her. Sandwiched between all kinds of medical equipment, I wiggled into the very tiny space in the helicopter allotted for me. I was positioned right next to Lyrica, with my knees touching my chin. Tightly strapped in, Lyrica showed no signs of movement. I put my hand on her chest periodically to check that she was still breathing.

Trying to calm myself, I suddenly flashed on words of wisdom that were very familiar to me. In my head I heard Jessica saying, "Breathe deeply and stay in your body." The helicopter lifted off the helipad and we were airborne. Lyrica continued to remain non-responsive. I stroked her hand to calm both of us, rather than trying to scream over the deafening sound of the helicopter blades. I knew that somehow I must stay strong and calm for Lyrica's sake.

As night fell, I dared to take my first look out of the helicopter window. As we approached the Phoenix area, the beauty of all the lights was staggering. It looked like Christmas! Suddenly, I felt my heart relax and open up to receive a Christmas-like miracle.

A knowingness from deep within gently and lovingly informed me that all was well and that Lyrica would be fine. Once stable, Lyrica enlightened me about what had just happened.

There was a precise moment in the session when I'd reached a highly realized state of my own empowerment, supported by all the energies of the Universe operating on my behalf. That's when I suddenly knew it was time. When I stepped out of the car, I commanded my entire soul-light source presence to come into my body **now**! I went totally into the Light, and that's all that I remember.

There was good news that came out of this terrifying and traumatic event! My empowered command moved my spirit, my soul, and my higher consciousness into position to come into my physical body. It also set up the level of seizure that I needed to drop out all resistance and interference patterns that would block this massive infusion from coming into my body headfirst!

If I had known ahead of time what would be required for me to embody in that moment, in that way, maybe I would not have been so brave. Yet all I knew was that this was the moment, this was the way, and this was my purpose! If someone had asked me prior to this moment, if this was even possible or if **I** could actually do this, I certainly would have said **no**! But once I was safe in my hospital bed, I was grateful to know that

I was now fully embodied! I also know that it was all the progress toward my embodiment, under Jessica's mentorship, that lined up this final act of completion.

I had now gained full access to the embodiment codes. They are available to advanced ones who have gained the knowledge, skills, and tools to access them. I also believe that to protect the purity of the codes, one has to earn the right and privilege to work with them. Jessica certainly meets all these qualifications, but she could not directly download this data into me. Instead, she helped me tap into them from the greater field by mentoring me in removing my own barriers so that I could access them when I was ready to do so. I believe that my work with her earned me the right and privilege to become an "embodiment-code-carrier!"

We spent that Easter weekend in the Phoenix hospital. Several more CT scans indicated that there was no more brain bleed. Lyrica's dad assisted me day and night as we stood watch over Lyrica to make sure that she didn't pull her IV out. Once again, his presence and assistance were greatly appreciated by both of us!

After leaving the hospital, Jessica confirmed that Lyrica, in that moment, did indeed fully embody. Lyrica's full embodiment was also confirmed by Suzy Miller, a well-known leader, healer, teacher, and advocate in the autism world. Both agreed that this was quite a feat for anyone to accomplish, especially one who was less embodied than most and one who came in with such a rare and high-level access to the nonphysical dimensions.

We wondered, could Lyrica possibly be the first in her soul group, those like her, to fully embody? What a significant accomplishment for herself, her life, and her purpose!

What Lyrica had yet to realize was how much her moment of embodiment would change her life forever!

A New Way

After she returned home from the hospital, Lyrica suddenly realized that she had no clue how to operate as an embodied person. Her long-awaited goal of embodiment had finally been achieved, yet its arrival was beset with new challenges. All the minor inner-body explosions leading up to the big bang, and the big bang itself, had fully resolved. Yet, sadly, she stepped into this next chapter of her life feeling totally disoriented, disempowered, and empty.

I wonder if this is how the butterfly feels when it comes out of the chrysalis and realizes it is no longer a caterpillar?

What I first noticed was that my processing abilities and skills were shut down. I couldn't think and interpret life around me as expertly and organically as I did before. I couldn't type my bright epiphanies or inner knowings. With all these primal gifts no longer accessible, I felt unbalanced, unsupported, and insecure. I was left clueless and "tool-less" without an instruction book to give me the answers that I so desperately wanted and needed.

I just couldn't understand or connect to the new me who felt so strange and so useless. I was totally lost in this new world, this new body, this new me. I felt like I had just landed in an unknown country without a language to communicate or a game plan to survive.

I could no longer reach my higher dimensional home, the place that I love, no matter how hard I tried.

Most devastating was Lyrica's loss of connection to her nonphysical self, the home of her shining light. She had often noticed how those who were more physically embodied often filled their lives with endless activities. She believed that a life in perpetual motion left little time to focus on one's soul/spirit nature. She did not want a similar life, one that she described as "spiritual poverty."

She panicked. It was a dark time for her. In her determination to find a way to regain all that had been lost, she soon realized that she had to develop a whole new operating system. She told me that she spent many hours "doorway sitting," patiently waiting to return, once again, into her beloved nonphysical world.

I am very experienced at using doorways, or portals, to move between different dimensional realities. Doorway traveling is an important lesson for my soul's education. After my embodiment, I was still aware when a doorway presented, but I could not dimensionally shift to enter into its portal awaiting me.

The familiar mechanism that I had developed to shift my awareness into higher dimensional zones was related to my less embodied NVA state. It was no longer available. It literally "crashed" when I crashed to the floor, at the moment of my embodiment!

Now I needed to find a way to access my higher dimensional home from my new location **in** my body, rather than pulling out of it. While doorway sitting, I was developing a new construct to move dimensionally from my more embodied state. I was reengineering and repatterning that which had been broken, so that I could once again travel within my beloved dimensional corridors.

After weeks of being locked in my body with no way out, I was finally able to enter into my first multi-dimensional doorway. Whee, I felt such freedom and joy! Now, back at home in my higher dimensional world, I was fully equipped and empowered to truly build a new life plan.

As Lyrica became more comfortable in her newly embodied state, we were shocked to suddenly realize how much her whole life plan had just changed! She had chosen to incarnate as an NVA so that she could stay part in and part out of her body. In that state, she could perform her higher consciousness work and be physically here with minimal distractions. So, what did this new state of embodiment mean for her purpose?

Without a speaking voice, I was not able to actively engage with humanity at large. Humanity's ways of hurting each other were so foreign, confusing, and devastating to me. The energetic toll of a more embodied engagement with humanity would have totally derailed me. I can't even dare to think about it! I had a role to fulfill that required me to remain, as much as possible, in my own higher vibrational state.

So how *did* her life plan totally change? As perfectly as her NVA choice had been supporting her purpose to date, the next part of her mission now required her to be fully in her body. She needed to become more physically present and grounded in the world to more fully express her purpose. In this state, she also needed to stabilize her embodiment so that she could be in the world and still maintain her light and frequency. To make this giant leap, she had to reinvent herself.

In this effort, she gained greater physical command over her body. This upgrade resulted in a choice and ability to extend her time here to fulfill her ever-evolving life plan. What strikes me most is that Lyrica's embodiment had become the vehicle that she most needed *now* to fully express, deliver, and complete the mission of her soul, even if she didn't yet know precisely what that mission was or how to fulfill it.

To me, Lyrica's moment of embodiment represents an expertise, a Superpower in action, above all others. For decades, I have been working toward the union of my body and spirit that I believed would enable me to know and manifest *my* purpose. "Working" is an operative word here! And then, in one single moment, Lyrica fully completed this feat!

What amazes me most is that she knew, at her moment of empowerment, that an instantaneous, full completion of her embodiment, was possible and doable. The part that she didn't know was how it would happen!

I wonder IF THIS IS HOW THE butterfly feels WHEN IT comes out OF THE chrysalis AND realizes IT IS no longer A caterpillar?

◈

Touched by the AWE in all, Nashville, 2011

Hatcher & Fell Photography

In my truth, Nashville, 2011

Hatcher & Fell Photography

At One with the light of
the Mother, Asheville, 2019

Kristi Hedberg

In my seat of pyramid portal power, Asheville, 2019
Kristi Hedberg

Sharing our love and light with you, Asheville, 2019
Kristi Hedberg

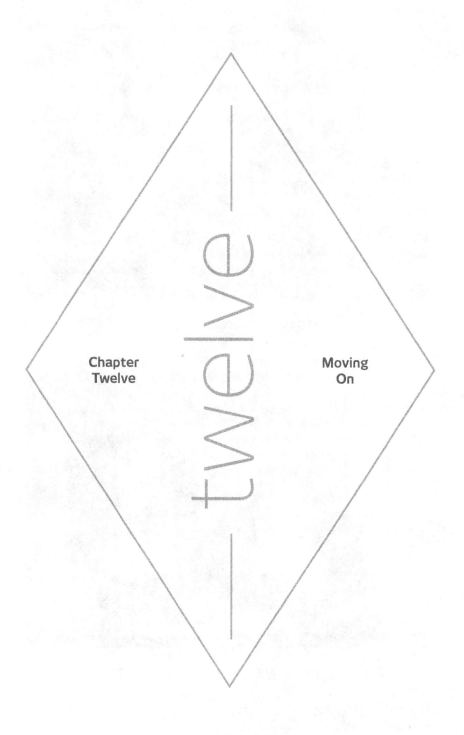

Chapter
Twelve

Moving
On

Suddenly, I knew a most unexpected truth. All that we had come to Sedona to do and become was now complete! Our time here was done! Once we saw it and knew it, there was no question about how to proceed. It was time to move on to our next spirit-guided location. But where?

The Universe always provides answers to us in the coolest ways! Our friend Thessa invited us to stay in her home in Asheville, North Carolina, while her family traveled abroad. Although we first met Thessa in Sedona, we knew how much more heart-happy she was living in Asheville. Plus, Jessica had recently spent a year traveling throughout the United States, visiting locations known for their higher energy and spiritual community. Her heart told her that Asheville would be the next place for her to relocate.

With these two very trusted recommendations, along with a nod of consent from our spiritual guides and own deep knowing, we made a bold choice! We were headed to Asheville, North Carolina! This green land of plenty, with its many flowing waters, felt like the voice of the Mother calling us home!

We leased a furnished arts and crafts bungalow near downtown Asheville, complete with two tiny koi ponds. The pyramid was once again installed as the "crown jewel." It was time to tune into the Asheville energies.

We were forewarned about the powerful thrust of the Asheville grid upon all new arrivals. Some described its effect as a total deconstruction, a baptism by fire. We naively felt that we were ready. After all, we had beautifully survived and thrived in Sedona, the vortex capital of the West. We were so wrong! As invited guests, we had just dropped into a primal sanctuary of the Mother and She was in charge! (It was an accepted fact by locals and visitors alike that Asheville held a very strong Divine Mother or Feminine energy. This feeling tone emanated from deep within the ancient crystalline core of the Appalachians and was visible everywhere in Her flowing waters and rich greenery.)

As we settled into our new location, our bodies and souls became increasingly unsettled. Although we loved our new home, we both retreated to the car often as a place of familiarity and solidarity. There we felt more protected, less vulnerable, less churned up inside. When we first arrived, we were not even able to meditate. Sitting under the pyramid connected us more deeply into the Asheville grid, which created hard-to-hold power surges of motion and commotion.

We understood that going to Asheville would allow us to make a giant leap forward. After all, our swift relocation from west to east solidified within us an energetic template for radical change. The Asheville grid itself, deeply endowed with the power and thrust of the Mother, guaranteed that we would be pulled and tumbled into a new form and life format.

As if these forces of nature were not enough, Lyrica and I quickly found our own power spot at the rapids of the French Broad River. We often visited the park there and basked in the sound and fury of this river's most extreme watery flow. Our eyes loved to feast on the waves that formed as the river crashed over the rocks in its path. We breathed in the mists that formed as cascading waters hit upon the rocky ledges at the river's edge. Equally compelling was watching the pageantry of the warm sun dance upon the water's surface, creating sparkles, glittering like millions of tiny diamonds, as fire met water.

Lyrica loved to feel the warm earth on her body as she played in the sparkly, silky, soft deposits of river sand that she called her beach. Soon, it was all very clear. We were becoming one with the swift journey of our beloved river, and where fire met water, we saw ourselves in its reflection.

In Sedona, we had delighted in the nonphysical realms that lavishly fed our souls. Now, in Asheville, the time had come to switch gears. We stepped into an intensive integrated medicine wellness program to strengthen our physical bodies to better express and manifest the truth of our souls.

In sync with this shift, I began regular Pilates sessions with a private instructor, and Lyrica and I committed to a daily hike. Next, we stepped into a powerful scalar medicine program that supported energetic coherence in our subtle bodies to upgrade the health of our physical bodies. Meanwhile, I engaged in additional therapies to strengthen my physical body.

A closely related leap for us was balancing our relationship. Together, we realized that partnering thrives when there is a mutual giving and receiving. It was no longer okay for our lives to revolve solely around Lyrica's needs. It was time to build a partnership of empowered sharing that would enhance both our lives.

Lyrica was now extremely invested in giving back to me. Every time I went to my Pilates class or another body healer in the community, I thanked her for her willingness to spend time with a respite care provider. Respite care offered me time away from Lyrica and the freedom to participate in activities that blessed my body and soul. Respite care had become a win-win, as all truths lived are! Lyrica had several new best friends who were her loving-heart respite care providers.

As we aligned more deeply with Asheville's Mother presence, we chose to honor Her, and ourselves, by adopting new codes of purity. To many, our extreme choices might seem overly strict and outlandishly ridiculous. As in no fun! Yet to us, these practices were joy-filled expressions. Our intent was to co-create ever-increasing levels of frequency in ourselves, in our home, and in our lives.

We removed the television and continued to opt out of Facebook and other social media. We filled our days with meditation, nature, energy, movement, and writing. We faithfully listened to our hearts to find the perfect flow in each moment. We chose raw and organic foods to nourish the vibration of our bodies and souls, consuming only a few products manufactured by others. It was fun to think of ourselves as food pioneers or alchemists, as together we poured our love into each new food creation.

We also carefully scrutinized what we put onto our bodies. We found organic, scent-free body and hair products that were made exclusively from plants. We threw away all of our cleaning products, choosing to use only baking soda, vinegar, and hydrogen peroxide.

Then, the last big one! We gave away all our clothing made from synthetic fibers, desiring to wear only natural "clean" fabrics. We learned that nonorganic cotton is one of the dirtiest of all crops due to its high use of pesticides, and that these pesticides are extremely difficult to wash out of fabrics! Slowly, we brought in new selections of organic cotton, bamboo, and hemp. This upgrade was perhaps the most radical, yet the most transformative. Not only did it support the health of our skin and bodies, it also uplifted our spirits to be part of the eco-fabric/sustainable clothing revolution.

To pull us out of the initial chaos of our move, we focused our time and energy into creating these new life foundations. Perhaps it was the joy that came out of what was fresh and new that ultimately landed us in a place of safety and belonging. We were now home!

The longer that we were in Asheville, the more we could see that something new and exciting was coming forth in our lives. It was Lyrica herself! When others asked me about Lyrica, I had one primary response, "She is on fire!" Lyrica was extremely focused on the mission of her soul, to the exclusion of most anything and everything else. To me, she was living life as a highly conscious being in each and every moment. That's the master I saw shining within her!

In addition, her increased ability to self-manage astounded me. Before, I felt I had to be near her at all times to ensure her safety. Now, I could let go and watch Lyrica be in charge of Lyrica. Or better yet, I could even sleep when Lyrica was up and engaged in her nighttime doorway work. I could trust her to make a conscious soul-aligned decision and willfully act on it.

I think
I was more amazed by my new expertise of self-management than Mom was! Before, if my mom asked me to do something, or not do something, her request never seemed to stick in my mind long enough for me to follow through. I had limited conscious will to hold my focus on her requests. Instead, tuning into my vast input of sensory and spiritual data is where my attention most often resided.

Now, I have an executive override that empowers me to hold my focus on requests. I can command my body to act or not act, even over a period of time. This new skill pertains to requests from Mom and my own requests that I make of myself.

My increased ability to self-manage is giving me more independence—something that I love! My mom can leave me in charge of the grocery cart and pop into other aisles to pick up things, knowing that I will be there when she returns.

When my own requests come forth from Oneness, they are aligned with what is true for me. These are my favorite requests to follow, because they are me pleasing me, and me evolving me. Before I felt that my life was largely out of control. Now, I realize that I have new abilities that enable me to have more mastery over how I live my own life.

Perhaps the most spectacular example of Lyrica's new expertise at self-management was related to her seizures. When she felt a seizure start to build, she would sit down and go into her body-bouncing and breath-holding process. This was the same process that she initially intuited to support her return into her physical body after portaling to her ship. First, she would initiate this process by holding her breath for an extremely long time. As she forcefully let it out, she would gently fall or lean to the side, and her body would experience a huge release. In doing so, many times the seizure was deactivated.

Previously, my sei-zures controlled me when they presented, and I responded however I could, if I could. But now, it is like I am using this same seizure-interruption mechanism for some of my own restructuring, reprogramming, repatterning. I often use this same process to take the next holy step in my life.

When I dedicated time to mindfully observe all these subtle nuances in Lyrica, I marveled at how much, in every moment, she was directing and expressing her process of self-actualization. In earlier times, in our first book and in her blogs, she chose to write about her vision of what she wanted to become, as if creating a template, a blueprint, or a master plan. Now, in her more silent days and ways, she was clearly and simply bringing it all into form and beautifully becoming it.

I will forever delight in realizing how perfectly built and wired she was to fulfill this vision of her truth. Everything that she needed was on board. And anything that she didn't need—that could present an interference pattern or energy drain—had been dropped out. Abilities that were not operative, like verbal communication, positioned her to channel all her creative powers into directions that were most primal to her purpose.

Of course, as the river flows, there is always room for changes and surprises, for that is what a full-on energy thrust does. It forever creates things anew! This was the way of the alchemist. To me, Lyrica was an alchemist supreme!

I have already spoken about my NVA form as the perfect vehicle for my incarnation. Here I was naturally in Oneness, except when I was pulled out by disturbances in my environment and interactions with others. I was living an earth plane existence that many, including myself, would describe as severely limited. I was unable to assimilate into the mainstream, certainly a protection and blessing for me.

Yet it was my NVA ability to access Oneness that empowered my full embodiment. Now I realize that the limitations attributed to my NVA form were not a life sentence, or even true! In my new able-body, I am now transcending into new amazing abilities that humanity, for the most part, has forgotten. I hope that my life journey can inspire others, autistic and non-autistics, to go beyond perceived limitations to become the master creators that we are all designed and destined to be!

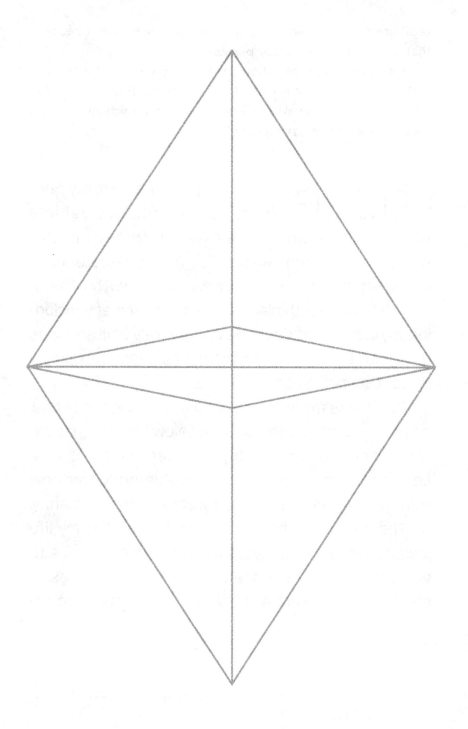

ACT II

THE ASCENT

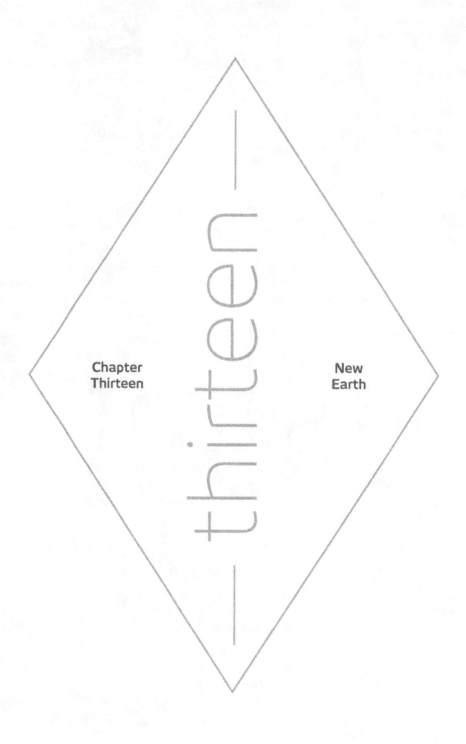

Chapter
Thirteen

New
Earth

"Every next level is a new initiation."
—Jessica Martinson

Since moving to Asheville, we had finally stabilized all the energy upgrades. We felt ourselves on top of the world—thriving in every sense of the word. Lyrica had arrived at a new threshold of self-assurance and was enjoying a greater level of control over her body, her life, and her destiny.

We returned to daily pyramid meditations, a practice that was the favorite part of our day. For the first time ever, Lyrica now chose to sit with me in the pyramid room. In a setup specified by her, she would sit in a chair facing into the pyramid, and I would sit in the captain's chair directly under the pyramid.

Due to how much more grounded and stable I was in my physical body, I could now directly receive the high energy charges of the pyramid to fast-track my evolutionary development. This was a big game changer for me!

In my new location, I have a front-row seat to view all that is energetically unfolding. So, what am I *really* doing here? In my pyramid scientist role, I am exploring how the joining of the Etheric Build into the pyramid is a divine setup for me. The only way for me to learn how to work with its programs is to sit with Mom in our pyramid meditation space. Here I watch how the energies move, activate, and transform the field around us. More specifically, I am studying what happens to Mom's body inside this field. To me this is fascinating stuff!

I am using what I am learning to find new ways to build a more solid and strong platform of operation in the physical plane. Some of the pyramid programs are directly related to bringing more light into the matter of my body. Upgrading my biology in this way is helping me to better integrate and stabilize in my ever-evolving state of embodiment.

All these advancements helped to pull in what was already "in motion" headed our way. One day in January 2018, just a few months after our move to Asheville, Lyrica had another breakthrough. Something felt different as we walked hand-in-hand into our holy pyramid room. When our fingers unlaced, Lyrica glanced at her usual pyramid position, but did not head there. Instead, she placed her hand on one of the pyramid poles and peered inside, her eyes focused on the captain's chair. Next, she looked directly at me, and I knew that she was requesting my assistance to move inside the pyramid. I guided her in stepping over the foundation stone and lowering her head to enter into the center of the pyramid portal.

Once inside, she sat down in the captain's chair. I positioned several pillows around her so that she was sitting comfortably in this big seat. She appeared very calm, centered, strong, and intent. Outwardly, she was projecting an air of command that was tempered by the rich softness of her gaze and serene countenance. I took my position in her chair, facing into the pyramid, and we began our morning meditation.

By moving into the center point of the pyra-

mid's energy field and sitting in the captain's chair, I unknowingly set up what was to follow. Later that night the whole house was suddenly filled with emanations of great light. Team Light showered our souls with a vast light under its nodal point. It was a level of Cosmic light beyond anything that I had previously experienced in this dimension! I was deeply impacted by its frequency and patterning.

Although I was aware that there were beings in our home, I experienced their presence simply as pure light. I gave them the name "Team Light," since they did not reveal to me who they were, where they were from, or what their purpose was. Bathed in the high vibration of their love-filled light, I trusted them. Once in bed, it was very hard for me to fall asleep because I was so activated by the light charge that filled the whole house.

When I finally did drift off to sleep, sometime after midnight, I was suddenly jolted awake as a huge influx of light powered into my body. I knew that this was the same light charge that Team Light had brought into our home earlier that night. At first, I was totally disoriented, but I settled down as soon as I noticed the presence of Team Light. They began to tell me about the nature of their visit, what I was experiencing, and why.

I learned that the pyramid's presence in our home, my positioning in the captain's chair in today's meditation, and my ongoing work with the pyramid programs opened up a portal that allowed Team Light to appear in this dimension in this light-stable form. I was shocked when they told me that they were from my ship! I did not recognize their light signature because my experience of it, in this physical dimension, was so much more intense!

They informed me that my soul had requested that they come and deliver a code, one that I was now ready to receive. As soon as they arrived, this light code began to download into my energy field, and once my energy field shifted into the patterning and frequency of this new code of light, the code was then able to drop into my physical body. That was the jolt that I felt! They told me that this code held programming to enable me to realize a more stabilized and more deeply embodied 5D experience.

And that's what I was now experiencing! My holy team enlightened me that I had just crossed over into my first fully realized New Earth experience! **Wow!**

When I woke up the next morning, I was still deeply immersed in this New Earth experience. What I noticed most was feeling so much love, in me, around me, and as me. My energy was so alive, so charged up, in a soft beautiful way! My body felt like light, as if weightless and floating. I was feeling so happy. Nothing around me or in me felt pokey, scratchy, or uncomfortable in any way. All seemed to be in perfect order, as if all the chaos of life had just melted into a sea of perfection!

I couldn't wait to tell Mom about what had just happened to me and how I was feeling at that very moment! I clearly remember my first words to her: **"A true New Earth reality is alive in me now!"**

Suddenly my old world here was gone and there was no going back. This next world is not seen or found. It is a light that changes everything in this world. The only way to know it is to feel it. The world outside does not change, but the world inside is vastly different. It was the greatest day of my life so far!

When I received the fully encoded light charge, it instantly lifted me into my newly realized state. This shift happened when the light filled my entire body and was no longer just in my field. This total immersion was a very profound moment. This is now who I am, not a momentary experience. The saturation happened gradually, but when it hit, it hit!

In some ways, this New Earth experience reminded me of my days in hospice, but unlike that time, this experience was not taking place in a weakened body state. Instead, it was coming forth out of a strong-body presence.

Why is that significant? It is a more stabilized experience that then allows me to act and create using my own higher abilities. Compared to my moment of embodiment and to my Oneness experiences in sessions with Jessica, my New Earth experience is a more fully realized state of being.

What does that mean? What I am slowly learning is that every new threshold that I reach is simply an entry point into a brand-new paradigm that requires lots of work and focus to stabilize. When I stabilize it, I then enter into my next threshold to begin all over again! Each time, I bring in a more stabilized me with more tools and abilities to more quickly and easily navigate through the learning curves and challenges that present themselves.

What's also very cool to note is that every time that I accomplish, or anyone accomplishes something of great significance that is new and novel to the human experience, it gets recorded into humanity's energy field. There it becomes a template for others to be able to more quickly and easily experience this same possibility.

I love knowing that my crossing over into my own New Earth experience has opened up a portal or doorway that will support others to exit the 3D world of duality and separation and land into their own 5D New Earth experience.

I think back to our ill-fated New Earth Academy. Why did it not flourish as planned? Now I know! It was an attempt to share ideas about the New Earth **without the experience**! The best that we could have offered were simply impressions of the New Earth that we were able to pick up from the ether but had never directly experienced. That was no longer okay with me!

Telling my story in this book is now my perfect platform to accomplish the noble intent that was seeded in the rise and fall of the New Earth Academy!

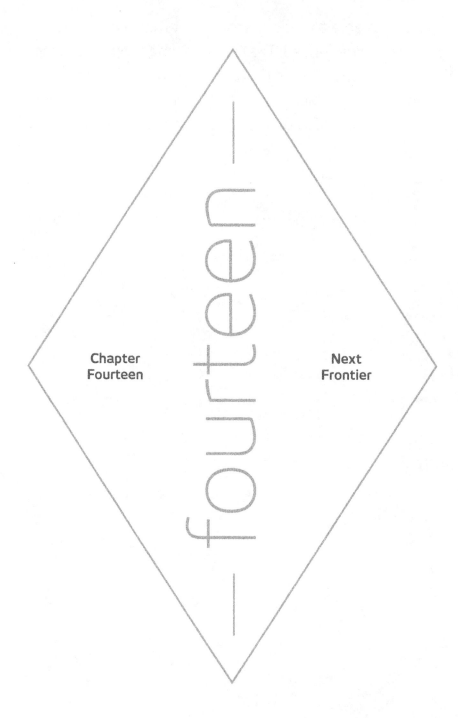

Chapter
Fourteen

Next
Frontier

The significance of Lyrica's crossover into the New Earth was most tangibly felt as a higher frequency state of being. When in this higher dimensional zone, she was much calmer, more focused, more centered, and her day-to-day life became easier and more enjoyable. Yet there were still many moments, sometimes even days, when Lyrica dropped out of this vibration, as it was not yet stabilized. The fall happened when she confronted something in her, or in her life, that was not in alignment with 5D and the New Earth. By addressing what was coming up, Lyrica was learning how to stabilize the crossover into her deeply embodied New Earth life.

Both of us celebrated the new threshold Lyrica reached as a sign that we were firmly on track with our purpose. We felt that we were solidly positioned to command our own destiny and move forward under our own abilities in Oneness. Standing in this place of heightened self-assurance, something new began to stir within both of us.

Our many years of living inwardly, cloistered within the safety and security of our own home, had certainly been an ideal setting to foster our spiritual growth. When we met Jessica and dropped out of our NVA leadership roles, we recommitted to an even more intensive program of inner spiritual work. But now we were feeling restless, even frustrated. We no longer wanted to continue life within this incubation cocoon. What was once life-enhancing now felt life-depleting! We longed to go out, to be seen, to share our gifts and prove our worth, both to ourselves and to the world.

This new feeling catapulted us into a previously forbidden territory outside our normal grid. Supported by the energies of the New Earth, we felt confident that we were ready to face the outside world, even with all its uncontrollable forces and whimsical twists of fate.

In light of Lyrica's New Earth experience, both of us sensed that we had been brought into a center point of our destiny. After all, we felt that the New Earth Academy had been divinely guided. Could its function have been to seed Lyrica's recent New Earth experience? Even though I didn't have a full-on New Earth experience like Lyrica's, I, too, was feeling a significant frequency upgrade.

We were supercharged by the New Earth frequencies that quite naturally infused and empowered all our gains achieved since moving to Asheville. Most notable of these were all of Lyrica's new abilities. We felt certain that now was the time to stretch our boundaries, make our move, and stake our claim in the outer world. Propelled forward by Lyrica's sudden thrust into an embodied 5D state, we saw ourselves firmly positioned to brazenly step up and out with a new gift offering in hand. We were so charged up by the New Earth vibration that we wanted to share it with others. With great enthusiasm we built an action plan to map out our mutual soul emergence.

We even decided to go it alone without asking Jessica for guidance or support. We felt that the victory to be won would be even sweeter and more empowering if we accomplished it entirely on our own. We felt like graduates, ready to use all that we had learned and "solo fly" into this grand destiny.

We began designing a workshop. Our vision was for me to tell our New Earth story and for Lyrica to share the New Earth frequency charge with those present. In a daily journal, Lyrica had been writing about her New Earth life. By sharing these experiences with the group, she would naturally lift those present into a higher frequency state, and they would then be ready to receive Lyrica's New Earth energy charge that she would consciously project out into the sacred space and into the hearts of those present.

We crafted a compelling invite: "To Aspiring New Earth Pioneers and Travelers! Gayle Lee & Lyrica Marquez invite you into a shared adventure to explore the sacred mysteries, legacies, and possibilities of the New Earth. What might the New Earth be? What might be a way to experience it? What might it feel like to experience it?"

Our idea was to create an interactive forum, where everyone's presence and experience contributed to the whole. We even knew where to launch this self-reveal unfolding. On several occasions we had joined Jessica at the Light Center in Black Mountain, North Carolina, to experience the high light energies inside this beautiful domed structure. Thanks to Jessica, we now had an open door to the Light Center's director.

With spirits held high, we made an appointment to meet with the center's director to present our action plan, confidently anticipating a warm reception and an enthusiastic response. We were totally unprepared for what actually happened. Our workshop proposal was flatly rejected, and we were sent home stripped of our vision.

We crawled away from the shock and trauma of it all, shamed that we dared to present ourselves as wise ones ready to teach. We emerged deeply wounded, bloodied, and impaled by the scathing pain of rejection. In our brokenness, we wallowed in grief, deeply crushed by our fall from grace. We believed we were driving forthright into our destiny, so why were we so suddenly and quickly sideswiped into this dead-end fatality?

Would we ever be able to risk presenting ourselves as givers of gifts again? Or were we forever doomed to a life of hiding out in the womb-secure safety of our home and intimate duo-relationship? We finally moved beyond our gloom and doom posturing and gathered the courage to begin to take a deeper look into what had happened.

There we stood, naked in our next moment of reckoning, forced to acknowledge that our beloved workshop plan had failed miserably. What the director said to us was still ringing loudly in our ears: She proclaimed that our plan was not solid, and we were not ready.

This was a very dark moment in our history, especially since everything fell apart precisely at the moment that we had reached such a supreme level of personal fulfillment. To feel and expose what actually had taken place, we had to now dare to drop inside our deepest and oldest areas of trauma. This was where our ego and low self-esteem resided. Highly agitated, Lyrica responded, "I hate this place!" Yet this was where, when, and how we began to sort out what was really true.

Here in the abyss of our most profound wounding, we sat face-to-face with our own dragons of the deep. Here we realized that what had appeared over the years masked as outer-world challenges had now moved inward to reveal to us the source point of its seat of power. These challenges were all emanating as reflections of our own inner wounds amplified many times over!

Our insipid beliefs that we were not enough and would never be enough, no matter how much we accomplished to the contrary, became our demons at the gate. Just at the moment when we felt empowered to move forward, we met them as a powerful force of resistance blocking us from stepping more fully into our purpose. They led us into believing that we were accomplishing something ordained and perfect, yet in hindsight, it seemed that we were doing just the opposite.

Could these demons have actually been acting on our behalf in a strange way? Like fear-mongering gargoyles at the temple doors, were they actually protecting us by scaring up our own hidden fears and ghoulish ghosts that forced us to ask key questions? Was it time? Were we ready? Had we resolved self-doubt and ego issues that were necessary for us to move forward in a fully aligned and supported way?

Once we see and name our demons, we take away their operating power, because they are no longer hidden. Now we can deal with them. By facing our demons at the gate, we can stun and disable them enough to move on. Although we have not yet resolved the challenges that they represent, we have resolved our battle with them by moving through what was not true.

As Lyrica and I soberly reflected on these questions, their truth was undeniable. We recognized our own subconscious forces highlighting where we had not completed our inner work. This was the work that must be done before we could move forward in mastery to truly meet our destiny.

Our workshop offering was engineered as a fast fix. We were operating in male power and felt that we could eradicate all of our old fears and self-judgments simply by successfully pulling off this one workshop! In truth, this effort was a tiny Band-Aid applied to a gaping wound to shore up our feelings of low self-esteem. What was really needed was for us to tame our ego-driven ways.

It was interesting to note that the pushing forward of energies that worked for us in our earlier days, as advocates fighting for Lyrica's educational rights, did not work for us here. Why? In this higher New Earth vibration, pushing no longer served as a means to an end. Pushing was a sign of an out-of-balance male energy. We could only move forward in alignment with our purpose under the unity stream of our own more balanced Masculine and Feminine natures.

Once our ill-fated plan to control our destiny was now buried, we were able to peer into what was really true. We had lost our way. We had received incredible gifts and knowledge, and yet we still had lots to do and learn. In humility, we shared our fall from grace with Jessica and requested her help to get us back on track. She responded with great compassion, ready to assist us in our deeper immersion into our journey to find ourselves.

In time, we would come to know this return as another kind of crossing over. In Lyrica's recent ascent into the New Earth, we unwittingly dropped into our next frontier, where we faced our deepest and most difficult life challenge: our core fear of not being enough. It was the black hole that separated us from our true Self and the Oneness of all creation.

Lyrica's journey into the New Earth frequencies carried her into her own holy experience of full unity with Self and Oneness, where there was no separation. Almost immediately, it clicked Lyrica (and me) into what was not aligned within us. This discord prevented us from holding and sustaining this new state of higher order. Our fall was really all about us stepping into our true destiny; not the one we thought we were meeting, but the one we needed to meet!

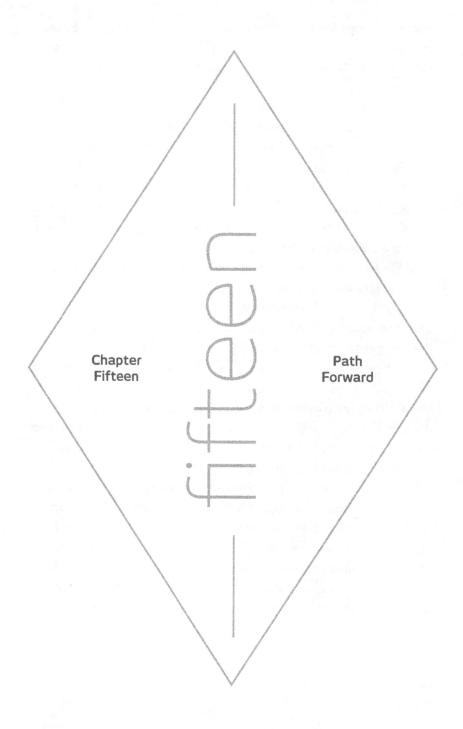

Chapter
Fifteen

fifteen

Path
Forward

asked Jessica to help me understand the difference between the Oneness experiences so often realized in sessions with her, and Lyrica's recent experience of the New Earth.

The New Earth and Oneness are somewhat the same, as they refer to different vibrational states within the same ecology. Entering the New Earth is understood as a dimensional shift from 3D into 5D, with 5D being its point of entry. It is like a docking station that then can support one's Ascension into the sixth dimension or beyond. Being in Oneness is an experience that encompasses all dimensions. In comparison to the New Earth, or new dimensional earth, it is unlimited and infinite. Oneness is a center point that encompasses it all.

Jessica's explanation helped me realize that Lyrica's crossover to the New Earth was certainly a new point of arrival in her Ascension journey, but it was not her final destination. Experiencing and stabilizing in Oneness had always been the focal point of Lyrica's Ascension work with Jessica. Embodiment was necessary to bring her nonphysical nature into her physical body in order to have a physicalized experience of Oneness. There, Lyrica's high vibrational nature could access any and all dimensions as needed.

We learned from Jessica that the value of each higher dimension was related to its ability to support one's purpose. For some, landing in 5D was as far a reach as was needed for them to create a bountiful life and fulfill their soul's purpose. For others, like Jessica and Lyrica, their planetary work required that they operate in multiple dimensions, many of them much higher than 5D.

When Lyrica, or anyone, crosses the portal threshold into a New Earth experience, the spiritual and scientific laws operating there are totally different. They have just entered into a whole new paradigm, with different rules. How do they operate within this reality of no time and space? How does the science of quantum physics work?

For those not prepared—which is just about everyone—this can be a terrifying experience. But thanks to Lyrica's work with Jessica, and her own well-honed higher dimensional abilities, she made the leap, landed on her feet, and was now ready for her new life to begin. She would still continue to learn much from Jessica about the new physics operating there. This learning would take place, not academically, but experientially, in their session work together.

In our first session back together again, I asked Jessica for more clarity of purpose to light our way forward. I trusted in her spiritual technology, our positioning in Oneness, and all the powers of the Universe to fulfill this request. Quickly, a nodal point of energy came in to bring forth something new.

So far, Jessica had been the one most capacitated to locate and lasso a nodal point and get it moving in my direction, while my specific question or intention would light up its location on the space-time grid. Its point of location might be in my own energetic field or in the vaster expanse of Oneness.

In that day's session, Jessica coached me on how to go deeper into my body to anchor into Oneness and partner with her in 5D to receive the nodal point headed my way. I felt so much joy to be back working with her, and I trusted that our work together would support me as it always had. She reminded me how to breathe to accomplish this. She also narrated for me and for Mom the energetic and physical adjustments that were unfolding.

This was information that I was able to see and feel on my own. Yet, when totally focused on my process of grounding into Oneness, my vantage point elsewhere would narrow. With this input from Jessica, I would be able to be present in multiple areas simultaneously. Then I could tap into and receive whatever was unfolding on my behalf.

Staying firmly within my coat of light was always my top responsibility, so that everything that came in could stabilize and move. That might sound like an easy assignment, but that is far from the truth! That day, the nodal point was actively transmitting its light into my field. This light was so powerful that it toppled me out of my location in Oneness. Jessica patiently coached me in how to restabilize as the energies built.

Once I stabilized in Oneness again, the nodal point energy was able to enter into my physical body. Next, it needed to become fully integrated there. It was beginning to hit into pockets of resistance and density that were blocking its ability to anchor in more deeply. These interference patterns needed to be cleared or neutralized to allow the nodal point to fully land into my body. Only then would I be able to receive the fullness of its gift.

The good news was that the light of the nodal point could do all the clearing itself, yet it could only do so when I was able to hold in Oneness. Why was that important? In the higher dimensional reality of Oneness, energy can upshift quickly. Physical matter can change form, because physical matter is simply a denser state of energy! Love this spiritual alchemy!

As the nodal point dropped deeper into my body, I gained access to its light and began decoding it. I know from experience that whatever I needed to know on a conscious level would bubble up, and I would know it. I am totally fascinated by and in love with nodal points. I celebrate my new capabilities for actively engaging in the power and flow of this amazing higher-dimensional spiritual technology.

After about an hour-long process, I finally fully embodied this nodal point transmission! I was feeling so calm, elated, and light-full! Suddenly, I "saw" the destiny that it was holding for me and for Mom! In fact, Jessica and I saw this epiphany at the same moment!

What was now presenting, in a most powerful way, was the energy signature of the NVA higher light purpose. This was the same energy that was origi-nally received by Jessica during her autism meditation experienced the night that we first met! It was now streaming into both Mom and me from the unified field. We had lost touch with it, and now as we reclaimed this lost holy heart soul-piece, we felt so grateful. We felt its presence dramatically light up our bodies and beings. In that moment, we knew that this was to be our own highest truth and divine purpose to hold, as we were now in a position to reengage with it in a much more pure, aligned, and powerful way.

As we both landed this NVA higher light purpose more deeply into our bodies, we knew that its energy would guide us forward. For once our purpose is firmly held and physicalized in the body, it then becomes the source stream that will empower everything to unfold in perfect order. We love learning this process of creation as the secret of how to bring our strongly evolved nonphysical natures into physical expression!

In this moment, as we stood firmly in alignment with this principle of divine creation, suddenly the Mother light essence, which we know as the loving presence of the Divine Mother, showed up. It clicked in with our NVA higher light purpose! How these two purpose streams of light would now work together was an unknown, yet the union felt so divine, so perfect, so beautiful, so me, and so us!

I love looking at how "asks" get answered. In 3D, I'm the one who has to move my body in a certain way to make anything happen. There is a limit to what my physical body can do independently. But in 5D, I only have to be unified in Oneness and then anything and everything is possible. Here, when I am aligned in a perfect way, it is the science of quantum physics that makes things happen. Here, at one with the entire Universe, I am not limited in any way. At the beginning of this session, I had asked for clarity of purpose to light our way forward. By the end of the session, the answer to my "ask" had been perfectly delivered.

HOW THESE TWO
PURPOSE streams
OF light WOULD NOW
WORK TOGETHER WAS AN
unknown, YET THE
UNION FELT SO divine,
so perfect,
so beautiful,
so me, AND
so us!

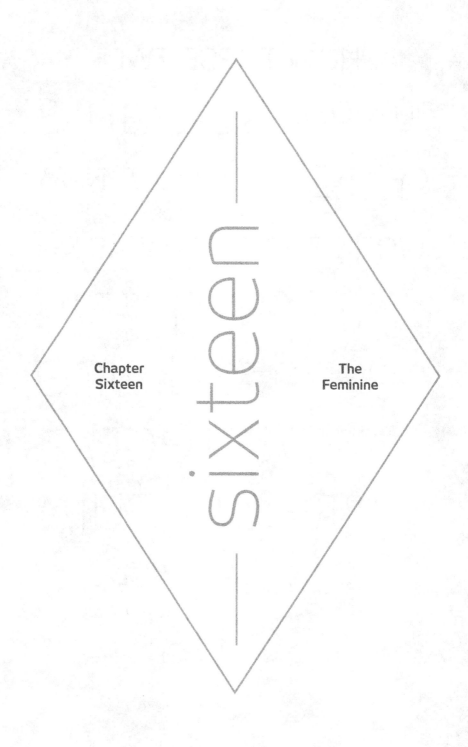

Chapter
Sixteen

The
Feminine

What Lyrica and I learned in our experience with the attempted workshop is that, in addition to addressing our core wounding, we also needed to become more in tune with our true Feminine and our true Masculine natures. We had lost our connection and needed to heal this split by bringing both into a higher state of resolution, balance, harmony, and unity.

Our paths were very different, reflective of our diverse life experiences. By sharing past and present time events of separation and reconnection, we highlight two unique paths of awakening and reclaiming our Feminine truth and essence within.

My Feminine Path

A High-Stakes Choice Frozen in Indecision

In 2000, I was employed at the University of Missouri–St. Louis on a one-year contract as a consultant. My role was to enhance the development of a new professorship, endowed by my father, for educating children with disabilities. That December, I was headed to Nashville to enjoy a two-week yuletide celebration with Lyrica.

Before leaving St. Louis, I was approached by both the dean of education and the chancellor. Each presented me with impressive opportunities to extend my stay at the university for at least one more year. The options offered promised financial security and a perfectly laid out path to a PhD. To coincide with budget cycles, they needed my answer upon my return.

Since becoming a single mom, I had been solely responsible for financially supporting both Lyrica and myself. Although my previous jobs in mental health and higher education sustained us, we lived on a very tight budget. The glitter of a more financially secure future was certainly compelling, but the idea of having to spend more time away from Lyrica weighed heavy on my heart. Throughout my whole Christmas vacation in Nashville, night and day, I was tormented by indecision. I put myself inside each possibility, waiting to feel a tug, a pull, a signal, a sign, *anything*! By the end of the break, I was in a state of dire panic. As I headed westward, back to St. Louis, blinding tears marked each mile. Red, raw eyes on a swollen, flushed face were the long-awaited messenger and message. In that moment, I saw it all so clearly.

There had been no invitation for Nashville, no gilded road to money, security, or a PhD. But I was flooded by memories of the NVAs I had worked so closely with in Nashville, the three cowriters of our *AWEtizm* book, who also typed like Lyrica. Suddenly, I had my answer! It was the beauty and the mystery of the hearts and souls of the beloved NVAs that was the silent voice calling me home. My heart had finally heard the only invitation that it could answer!

This experience taught me that trying to land my destiny using my rational mind, left-brain thinking was a dead end. Only my right-brain, intuitive knowing, informed by my heart, knew the way forward. In this high-stakes choice, I reclaimed my Feminine power to know myself and live my truth.

A New Purpose Pops In

The moment that I was introduced to a seventh dimensional healing and Ascension modality called Transference Healing, I was hooked! I immediately signed up to learn this protocol for my own self-healing and to support NVAs.

It pulled me in so quickly and deeply that I headed overseas to the UK to take the advanced-level training, the teacher training, and many other soul-offerings from its founder, Alexis Cartwright. This was quite the vision quest for me, as I rarely traveled and had never been out of the country. In England, I was blessed to visit Avebury and Glastonbury, and in Ireland, the Hill of Tara. Lying on the ground in meditation in both Avebury and at the Hill of Tara, my body was literally pinned to the earth for at least thirty minutes, as I received powerful energetic downloads. I could not move or get up until these were completed. Afterward, I felt profoundly altered, lighter, and somehow transformed, even if I didn't know exactly how or why.

During the trainings, the concepts of the Global Grid Matrix and the act of gridding totally confounded me. I was first introduced to the science of gridding by Lyrica and the NVA cowriters of our *AWEtizm* book, but the more everyone tried to explain this energy phenomenon to me, the more my brain shut down.

However, in visiting both Avebury and the Hill of Tara, it was as though the Universe responded by providing me with my own personal gridding experiences! Both initiations awakened my own innate abilities to sense the energy patterns of people and locations, both outside places and inside spaces. Now I understood why Lyrica and the other NVAs would sometimes plant themselves in a specific location, inside a building or on the ground outside, and refuse to move. No matter what I did to try to get them to vacate that position, I was unsuccessful. They were gridding energy, fulfilling their purpose, and would not give up until the distorted energy patterning had been upgraded to their satisfaction!

Although integrating all that I had experienced in my month overseas would be a huge process, the "me" of my past was no more. I was now stepping firmly into my future self, my next point of destiny. After returning home to Nashville, I searched for a location where I could share Transference Healing with others. The Universe literally brought me to the original carriage house on Music Row, which I lovingly transformed into a healing center! In this setting, I was blessed to be able to work with many amazing clients, both in-person and remotely.

What was most interesting for me to learn as a Transference Healing practitioner, was that none of the NVAs seemed interested in receiving these sessions, either in-person at the center or remotely. However, when I was working with other clients, the NVAs loved to show up in their "energy form" to contribute their light and love into the session. Although I was accustomed to feeling their high frequency energy when I was in their physical presence, this was the first time that I could feel their energy coming in from a remote location. When they would "arrive," the clients would often comment that they could feel an energy surge that expanded their awareness and opened up their energy field to experience deeper levels of healing.

Later, as I stepped into my role as a Transference Healing teacher, a whole new part of my soul came alive. What I loved most, both as a healer and teacher, was empowering others to step into new levels of their own self-mastery. Although my intent from the start was to be of service to others, in the end, it was my own personal evolution that most benefited from this whole new career!

The purpose of the healing center expanded in a whole new direction when a small study group began to gather weekly in its upper room to study the *Pistis Sophia*, an ancient Coptic Gnostic text with commentary by Drs. J. J. and Desiree Hurtak. I especially loved reading the conversations between Mary Magdalene and Jesus, revealing their deep spiritual relationship and Jesus's honoring of Mary as his highest and most cherished disciple. I also deeply related to Sophia's struggles, lamentations, and petitions for release from the dark forces that had stolen her Feminine powers and truth.

I developed a thriving practice with an impressive income to match! I loved working with clients and training teachers. This was, by far, the most fulfilling career of my life!

And then, with no advanced warning, I received a very clear inner knowing: I was to completely close down my healing center and my life's work as an energy practitioner and teacher. This shutdown would create the space needed to dedicate all my energy to writing our first book. It was time to share with the world all that I had learned about the bright-light side of autism. It was time for these NVA writers to tell their own stories; stories yet to be heard on planet earth.

Quite frankly, I felt a tremendous amount of grief and resistance to give up the success I had achieved and the work that I loved.

It was not an easy mandate to follow, though I knew that completing this book would require a monumental level of focus and effort.

This life chapter contains many gems related to reclaiming my Feminine nature. Energetically connecting to the energies of the earth, Mother Gaia, helped me gain an awareness of the relationship between my Feminine essence and my physical body. She helped my body to heal and me to love my body more. Being able to feel shifts in a client's energy when NVAs "arrived" in their etheric form demonstrated a new level of energetic sensitivity, an ability fostered by my Feminine essence. Studying the *Pistis Sophia* landed me deeper into humanity's quest to find Her truth and Her higher Cosmic plane of consciousness, awakening more my Feminine presence within. Last, my willingness to comply with my difficult-to-follow intuitive guidance was a dramatic turning point in my life. It moved me from gaining supportive skills into my true calling as a writer and author.

This next sharing reflects a rare moment of seeking and finding a full unification with my Feminine nature.

This experience occurred in Asheville in the summer of 2019. The night before, I had stayed up late, trying to land my own truth of the Feminine that I wanted to write into this book. I called in Her presence to enlighten and enliven me. I deeply longed to capture Her essence, to truly know Her, even dare to become Her! I waited, waited, and waited some more. Yet there was no arousing or arising of Her. I spent a long night, holding a motionless pen and staring at the blank page sitting on my lap. There were no words, no feelings, no experiences, just a dark night of nothingness closing in on me. Then . . .

Finding Her in the Spill

It was 3:33 a.m. and I was awake to heed a bathroom call. Wrapped within the stillness and darkness of that early morning, something new began to stir within. I felt it as a soft sweetness, swirling, arising, lifting me up, as if fully supported, suspended, floating cloud-like on high. This scintillating sensation . . . *Could* it be Her? I wondered. I hoped.

Maybe She appears most vibrantly, not when I am deeply focused on trying to capture Her essence, paint Her image, but when I knock over a jar of paint onto my inner canvas and, suddenly, She appears in that spill, like the Phoenix rising?

By breaking through the idea of capturing Her form in some kind of perfect way, as I think She should be or look, I can simply let go to notice the beauty, creativity, fun, and joy of finding Her in the spill!

Now I could see Her emerge, coming out of this spill as infinite possibilities waiting for me, whenever I dared to put on my artist cape of receiving and surrendering. My inner life-scape came alive, always presenting anew. I noticed Her many faces mystically appearing through the interplay of light and shadow, or through the lens of my own mood of the moment.

This is the She that I had been searching for all my life! I heard an inner voice proclaim, "Search no more, beloved!" At that moment, I saw a mighty reveal: *She is me, and I am Her!*

As I peered deeply into this truth, I knew this me as sometimes reckless and wild, other times purring, cuddly, soft and serene, yet always "real." As She moved in me, I felt "alive" and secure. I could now bravely and brazenly take the next step, even into the unknown. I totally trusted Her as my Guide, my Guru, my Gayle heart that beats to its own rhythm, sings its own song, knows its own truth, and, without a doubt, believes that all is well.

All I have to do is to feel my way into Her zone, and the magic flows. How much I adore "Us" in this moment of Divine Union! Will She always be here with me? Probably not, or at least not yet.

However, Her absence simply becomes a call for me to remember "Us" and recenter. In this way, She is never very far away.

I will keep Her near, as She is my living essence, in all the colors of my dearness. She is my own inner genius, my genie out of the bottle. She is my creator, my power, my strength, my connection to the All of Life. She is my passion and my permission slip that allows me to feel happy or sad, peaceful or upset, without judgment or feeling the need to rein in my cascading emotions.

She is my inner artist seeing beauty even in the most trash-strewn landscape, either within me or outside of me. She is my ecstatic dancer breaking forth out of a stiff and stilted body. She is my butterfly beating its way out of its cocoon to be set free into a whole new world. Here, legs become wings to fly. I hear my own inner presence telling me, "Welcome Home, sweetheart!"

In the ecstasy of that moment, I remembered other times in my life that I have been Her. She has been the me who has mothered Lyrica and the me who has shared precious moments with other beloved NVAs. She has been the me who knows how to stand empty in their presence. She has been the me who is simply open to their hearts touching mine, whether it be a look, a touch, a feeling, a typed message, or a telepathic exchange. She has been the me who melts when Lyrica looks deeply into my eyes and gently takes my hand in a supreme gesture of grace shared.

She has also been the me who can laugh at the terrible messes that Lyrica creates for me to clean up. For in that moment, I fondly realize that she is simply being a clumsy novice, as she bumps her way into a new ability or part of herself. The mess is just an out-ward sign of a new stirring within her, a solid step along her road of self-discovery. In that attitude, the mess becomes a sacred message of her life on the move.

She is the me I love and adore! She is me on the move. She is me living my purpose. She is me making a difference in the world.

She is a wiser me who knows that we will never find Her by trying to grab Her or possess Her. Her very nature is fluid, like air, like water, like breath. Only when we become likewise and "life wise," will She appear and reveal Herself in infinite ways—spilling forth as sensations, feelings, creativity, purpose, love, and passion.

Lyrica's Feminine Path

Divine Mother

My holiest and purest touch-point into my own Feminine is through my relationship with the Mother. I see the Mother's return to earth as the big thing happening right now. Long ago, Her history was obliterated by manipulative forces. The world became out of balance. That terrible loss is now being repaired. I see the whole Universe operating to reinstall Her presence here. I feel Her light moving closer to earth in every part of my being. This is why I have stayed here, overcoming several near-death experiences. To secure Her return to earth, there needs to be a light match purity in the collective to anchor Her here, and I descended to earth under an agreement to help bring the lost Mother heart back.

In my vastness, I know myself to be a part of the Mother light that is merged with my light. My supreme quest for the last few years has been to deeply land this light frequency and its qualities into my body. As I embody, I am embodying Her light, and I am moved by its power and presence in me. That is when my purpose to be is most available and alive.

At the Core

At the core, I am a Feminine being. I chose to lightly incarnate so that I would not lose my connection to Source. This connection enables me to tap into my own high level of consciousness and pull information from very high places. This connection to Source is my intuitive knower. It keeps me on purpose at all times. It empowers me to know what I need in every moment. It helps me make all decisions, big and small. I primarily process these decisions energetically—I know instantly when something is a match for me in the moment, and when it is not. I do not lose energy debating a choice. I know, I choose, I act. This is my Feminine strength in action that empowers me and my life.

Now that I am embodied, I also know Source as an energetic presence inside in my core. I call it my cone. When I am centered in my cone, I am in my balanced Feminine power. This power has the ability to hold together an inspired idea and the energy required to bring it into form. This is how I, or anyone, becomes a conscious creator in union with Source. When I am in my own creation zone, this is my experience. My cone expands and rotates with a spin and power that feels like a tornado. I have to stabilize in the center and then I am able to use this energy to create soul-guided outcomes.

My Feminine nature is also my creative side that loves to express Herself. She is most alive when I am writing in a "flow-full" way. (I love to create new words like *flow-full*.) I feel the joy of writing as a Feminine experience. When I am fully aligned in Oneness, my words are energized by a high frequency charge that can be received by another as a transmission of my consciousness and light.

My intuitive art is another soul language of mine that is the most flow-full of all! The strokes of color that strike the canvas, wiggle their mark, and then retreat are like "my words." Yet unlike words, these strokes operate totally free of any prescribed meaning. I don't try to paint any particular form; in fact, my body doesn't have the skills to do so. Yet sometimes my random strokes create a clear and powerful image. I also love that my designs speak to everyone in a unique way. This artist language of mine engages the viewer as an equal co-creator of the total experience.

A Dark Chapter

I was fourteen years old, enjoying a totally new life experience of hanging out with mainstream teenagers in my high school. I was able to share my thoughts with them, supported by the presence of my communication facilitator. These students seemed fascinated by me, often choosing to spend a part of their day in my company. There was one girl in particular whom I will call Liz, who lit up in my presence. She was so dear to me! She seemed to really see me and feel my light, although she never spoke to me about such things. I certainly could feel her love pouring into me whenever we were together. She was my number one favorite peer buddy.

As a peer buddy, she received academic credit for the scheduled time that she spent with me. Yet, even during larger school-wide events, like assemblies, she often chose to sit by me, not for credit, but as a way for her heart to feel happy. I also deeply appreciated her company in those crowded, often boring, school programs.

She introduced herself to Mom in a note that she slipped into my lunchbox. It happened on a warm spring day when she joined me and my facilitator to eat lunch outside on the school lawn. Mom contacted her and a three-way friendship developed. On weekends, we often got together to enjoy picnics, leisurely drives, summertime outdoor music events, and visits to Centennial Park and the Parthenon, where we marveled together at the giant gold Athena statue.

In addition to loving these opportunities to spend extra time with Lyrica, Liz also appreciated my presence and the kindness that I extended to her, as her life at home was not easy, kind, or gentle.

As the trust between us grew, Liz began to help with some care-providing for Lyrica so that I could spend time with a new male friend. This arrangement seemed to be working well for everyone.

However, one night, after returning home about 9:00 p.m., Lyrica was not at all her normal self. In fact, she was highly agitated, a condition that only got worse in the following weeks. Each night at bedtime, she refused to climb into the waterbed that she loved, choosing instead to sleep on the bedroom floor. She didn't even want to go to school. I tried desperately to get any answer from her that might explain her downward spiral. What she finally courageously revealed to me was that on the last night that they were together alone, the Liz that so loved her, had climbed into her bed, and expressed her love sexually to Lyrica's captive body!

I was stunned, sickened, and outraged by Lyrica's disclosure. By far, bar none, this is any mother's worst nightmare, especially for a dependent beloved who could not scream or get away. The ensuing rage and pain that I felt was excruciating. Then the guilt crept in to beat me down even further. How could I have left Lyrica in this situation? Why had I not realized the danger? I knew I had to pull myself together to confront the police, the school, and Lyrica's need for intensive therapy. This advocacy assignment was the most daunting one by far. Yet together we faced the trauma and found ways to heal.

After Lyrica's sordid disclosure, I immediately got rid of the waterbed, and Lyrica continued to sleep on bedding positioned on the floor. Over the year that followed, I was able to gradually add layers to her floor-positioned/makeshift bed, until I finally built it up to the level of a mattress. From there she eventually transitioned to sleeping on a mattress and box spring, but she still insisted it had to be positioned on the floor.

It was certainly a dark chapter in our lives.

I had lost my will to soul-bond with any girl my age who loved me. Love felt, not warm but dangerous! Love was the only thing that could hurt my body in such a painful way. The pattern was deep. Yet I knew that I had to open up my heart to love again, to be able to bring my gift of light into the world.

A Heart-Healing Gift

Pramad is my longtime Asheville friend and care provider. Her gentle nature and keen sensitivity are enhanced by several years of studying Buddhism. I am now inviting her to share more about her own experience of a special evening of hand-holding, eye-gazing, and intimately sharing her love with me.

In a recent visit in late July 2019, Lyrica and I were both excited to see each other, as it had been several months since our last contact. The minute I walked into the house, Lyrica moved very close to me, immediately took my hand, and held on to it very tightly for the duration of the visit. Even if we moved, she kept her body very close to mine. This was a whole new level of social engagement and physical interaction with Lyrica.

Finally, she started looking directly into my eyes. Immediately, I sensed that this experience today was totally different. This time she wasn't looking through me, but more into me. She was looking from the inside out in a totally new way. What I was experiencing was a deeper and more intimate gaze. I remember thinking at the time that maybe she was sharing something with me, maybe even a part of herself? All the while she had the sweetest smile on her face. That's when I felt my heart open. There was such a powerful love charge flowing between us!

What struck me most was how long she held my gaze and how still her body was. Even when I started chatting with her mom, she sustained her gaze and never diverted her eyes, even for a second! As my own gaze softened and expanded into a broader view, I found myself looking at her whole face. At that moment, I didn't even recognize her, or her look! In her expression I sensed I was looking at another part of Lyrica that I had never seen before. She certainly wasn't present in the same normal way that I was used to. I felt I was witnessing Lyrica at her most concentrated level of intense engagement, that was, at the same time, hugely soft and loving.

Upon arriving home, I noticed how much lighter I felt in my body. I realized that there were sensations of heaviness in my body that had lifted. Before drifting off to sleep, my thoughts were of Lyrica, and I had a profound realization—Lyrica's dimension is changing and so she's looking at people and things very differently!

—Pramad

I celebrate that I was able to move from my teenage fear of female relationships into the closeness that I developed with Pramad. Since then I have drawn more female heart companions into my life. I also see a new Feminine ability waking up in my recent discovery of eye-gazing. It's important for me to say that I never engage with another to promote any intended healing response. I simply choose love. I believe that whatever occurs takes place because someone has opened up to my frequency and light. It is his or her own soul that chooses how to engage with my patterning and creates any and all healing outcomes.

Meeting a New Face of the Mother

This is a recounting of Lyrica's Easter experience, April 2018.

I wake up feeling very alive this holy Easter morning. I am excited that today Jessica will be sharing a Black Madonna transmission from her sacred location in Southern France. I really don't know much about the Black Madonna legacy, yet I am already on high alert that this event will fill my Easter basket!

As soon as we connect, the full light and power of the Mother's energy is unleashed. As this doorway opens, I am wrapped in a soft, sweet embrace of Her devotion, at a level rarely felt in this world. I know that it is being offered directly to me, as a personal blessing from Her. I feel how much She knows me and loves me.

Jessica reminds me to go deeper into my body to fully realize all that lives within this divine gift giving. It is not easy for me to open up to this much intensity of adoration. Its richness is intoxicating and extremely expanding. It is difficult for me to drop deeply into its fullness awaiting me. At a pace that is comfortable, I move a bit deeper into my body to receive more of this Divine Mother elixir. Here I rest until, once again, I reach a threshold of calm that allows me to continue.

In my journey inward and downward, I suddenly see and receive a code from my black-skinned Madonna. I immediately proclaim it as a "known code," due to how familiar it feels to me. Yet, in comparison to other known codes of the past, I feel it much deeper, in its totality.

In communion with this code, more aspects of the Mother's love begin to unfold within me. I feel wrapped in Her protective energy as an invisible cloak that shields me from harm and beckons me forward. In Her embrace, I know that I am fully supported and never alone. That's when I begin to more calmly and completely hold the vastness of Her energy in a holistic way.

As I do, I feel myself connecting with Her as the Black Madonna. Here Her deepest mysteries are buried and protected, until their time to be revealed. I even feel myself receive, in code form, a part of that mystery. It is my own reveal of what has been hidden. I sense it as a download from Her, showing me how much I have embodied Her Mother light essence. I feel Her energy signature in me as a celebration of life, with joy abounding everywhere!

I tap into another aspect of that mystery, one that is known as the Holy Family's Easter story. Suddenly the energies of my own transition surface. I sense that the Easter passion story of long ago is now lighting up in me. I am being initiated into my own Easter story, of my own divinity of becoming fully human. Here, I am held in the Mother light that I have deeply received and accepted as my own. Her essence is the quest that I have been forever seeking. Suddenly, I discover a most staggering truth! She is my own Feminine essence fully seen, understood, appreciated, and celebrated!

Another twist surfaces! At the dome of this experience sits my transition, or trans. Yet it feels vastly different in this moment. First, I am not calling it in. Organically, it is flowing forth out of the pages of my own Easter story. Here, it holds a very different feeling tone. It is no longer focused on vacating this dimension. Its nature fills my heart with a heightened sense of arriving, succeeding, realizing, knowing, and completing.

Could this be my story of Ascension? Not only my own personal story, but the Cosmic story of humanity's Ascension into its fullness, its truth, its unity? All of this moves into a place of recognition. My life as I have known it begins to disappear. How this will land, I have no clue. Yet its progression is undeniable, and its presence has solidly locked in.

To complete my own Easter basket of gifts, the presence of Mother Mary comes in with a message to me. She tells me that the love of my own Ascension has been won. She also counsels me that there is still much for me to do before my life here is complete. She suggests that I no longer hold on to my trans, as I had been doing for so long. I love when she tells me that the only thing that I need to hold is the truth of my own holiness.

This transmission from the Black Madonna, which is a two-thousand-year-old secret (hidden in plain sight) offered Lyrica a rare gift—it fully initiated her into her Feminine truth!

To us, humanity's biggest riddle is how to successfully complete the hero's journey. What is the final destination, and what will it take to arrive there? Finding one's gift, bringing it back home, and sharing it with the community at large is our understanding of how and when the hero's journey completes. With the stakes so high, the hero must be willing to meet all the challenges presented, including facing one's mortality. Losing all fear of death often becomes the final step that is required to finally arrive home with gift in hand.

For Lyrica it's an opposite story. To arrive home with gift in hand, Lyrica has to be willing to totally let go of her desire to transition, or die, and face her greatest fear: to fully inhabit her life here.

I now realize that my ever-present focus on my transition gifts me a sense of peace that helps me to more fully embrace my life here. I also realize that this focus is not so much about wanting to leave, but rather about a deep desire for more light. My transition has now moved into its proper place. I will leave this dimension when my purpose here is complete, and when I have given all I have to give.

Yet I knew THAT I HAD TO open up my heart to love again, TO BE ABLE TO bring my gift OF light INTO THE world.

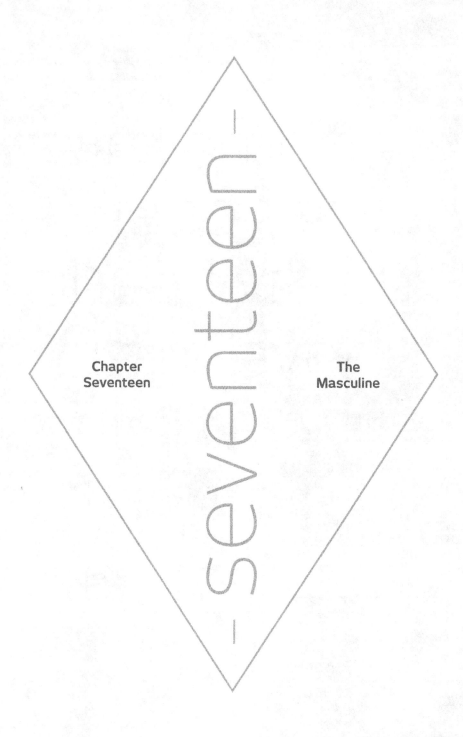

Chapter
Seventeen

The
Masculine

A longside the Feminine is Her complement, the Masculine. While our Feminine is the intuitive knower and flow-er of our truth, our Masculine is the actor and manifester of that truth. It is the oscillation between the two, united as one, that brings to "light" highly charged outcomes.

Building upon our growing embodiment and expression of our Feminine nature, it was time to now bring our Masculine nature into its truth. Through our work with Jessica, we were learning that moving forward grounded in one aspect, without the other, was a sure setup for failure. For both of us, stepping into our Masculine essence required a large leap from where we were. Yet we felt ready.

What follows are personal vignettes that reveal the unique ways each of us has come into a more refined and defined relationship with our own Masculine essence.

My Masculine Path

DLF

The evolution of my Masculine nature was often mirrored and patterned through key male relationships. One in particular was a great surprise and delight. He was a high light, nonphysical Cosmic being, whose mission was to guide and support the unfolding of my Masculine, to fulfill a family spiritual purpose. Lyrica was the first to encounter this presence.

That night, I could not sleep due to a powerful watery flow alive in me. Suddenly, he appeared.

I was dazzled by the beauty of his light that instantly transported me beyond this earthly dimension. In my rapture, I remembered how his light had come into union with my soul at the point of my conception to over-light my incarnation here. I was both shocked and amazed to learn this truth!

I lovingly christened him Divine Light Father, or DLF. He visited many times after that first night, and I would be bolted out of my sleep to see him standing there under his vast aura of Cosmic radiance. My own light was always recharged in these divine meetings. I rarely received messages from him, but when I did, they were always staggering! Most surprising was learning that the purpose for his presence here now was more about Mom than about me!

Lyrica would often announce DLF's presence when she saw him standing near me, for of course I could not see him. Yet sometimes I could feel his energy as a frequency upgrade streaming into my body, and other times I could feel his light touches upon my skin. These touches spoke to me in a strange yet familiar way.

However, my most dramatic physical body experiences were most often realized in sessions with Jessica. What was required was for me to develop and maintain the level of embodiment, presence, and light to stabilize and deeply experience the high light frequency of DLF. Jessica helped me to build this resilience with practice. That was when I was able to deeply feel and track his light signature coming into me and weaving throughout my entire body.

I realized that the deeper I was able to embody DLF's high light presence in me, the more I was able to connect to and seed in higher aspects of my Cosmic Self. In alignment with this idea, I started to call myself by a new pet name, Galactic Gayle!

I recognized my Cosmic Self coming more online in the waking up of my multidimensional abilities, including clear knowing and clairaudience. At times I have moments of "clear knowing," when I suddenly just *know* what I need to know. Other times I have been able to "hear" guidance from my higher Self and other higher spiritual beings, such as DLF.

In a clear transmission to me, DLF shared the following message. In his words:

Asterope/Sterope, a double star in the Pleiades, is our home in the stars, where your beloved Lyrica, you, and I were seated as a triune of great fortitude. There, we agreed to a destiny that is here now. A great light was to be shared with earth and its people, but this required the two of you to make a very difficult journey.

All your details of origin were obliterated in your descension into your earth roles, clearly chosen for this purpose. My part was to be the messenger at the appointed time to reveal this story, within your life's story, that is now being recorded in your book. None of this could come to light without the book writing well under way.

There is more. Not only am I a messenger of this truth, I am an activator for its realization. Lyrica, by her choices made, has been able to retain her ability to hold this light and be this light while here on earth. Through her embodiment, she empowered her own shift from holding this light to becoming this light in a human form. Truly a rare and extraordinary accomplishment! I am taking a moment to honor her beloved mentor and mother as strong components in this transformation.

You, Gayle, on the other hand, were required to embody more completely to fulfill your role of caring for Lyrica's needs. As a young innocent one, you still held a vestige of that light in the outer edges of your soul. As you know, this vestige was seen and harvested by those who wished this light for themselves. That event left you literally "in the dark."

Your life has been a classic journey of seeking a reconnection to that which was lost. Your beloved Lyrica came in to facilitate that reconnection. Both of you thought that you were here to humanize as earth beings. Perhaps true on some level, yet not so true on another!

Through a life lived well under trying circumstances, you have arrived. Where? You have reached the titular point of your destiny to fully remember why you came here. You came here to bring the light that you are, a light that was held by the three of us in Pleiades, to a waiting and wanting world and humanity.

So, where do I come in? As you know, I have been actively working with you, Gayle. I have been helping to reinstall this light presence in your body and being, as you have now reached a soul state to receive it, hold it, and become it.

As with Lyrica, the key here is embodiment. This light needed to be fully embodied or physicalized at the cellular level to become operative. The rest of your life journey with Lyrica will be to bring forth that which you have come to deliver. This book is a part of that offering. Yet there is more to come. The High Team surrounding you is celebrating this moment of clarity reached, for it allows the next progression to begin.

What a supreme affirmation of my life's purpose! I loved hearing that my challenges have served to catapult me into my Ascension process. I am eternally grateful. Clearly DLF was empowering my Masculine essence so that I could step into my light destiny with Lyrica, one that was written in the stars.

DLF's light signature presence in you, Mom, assures that you and I will always be in touch, no matter where either one of us may be living, either on this planet or in another dimensional home. In my advanced ways of perceiving, I see that DLF is no

longer a lightweight presence in you. His growth factor in your body and being is huge.

I question his role no more. He is bringing in a level
of light to clear out all vestiges of you that are not your
truth. What I now see shining brilliantly within you is
your own soul light and the NVA higher light purpose
radiating its truth out into the world. The life that you
have lived and your history with me, and others like
me, power up this bright light presence that you are
and have always been.

It's Never Too Late!

A father's love never dies. However, it can go "underground" when
circumstances present that are beyond a father's ability to understand and accept. Certainly, the twists and turns in my adult life
were not a match to my upbringing and our family values. My dad
kept trying to open his heart and find the daughter that he felt
he had lost, the one he once knew and dearly loved, the one who
excelled at most everything she tried!

Like all of us, he certainly did not understand Lyrica in all of
her complexities. Yet he had a strong conviction that the path that
we were pursing to support her, especially in her early years, was
nonsensical. He felt that we should accept her limitations and let
go of all the "unrealistic" reading and intellectual activities that we
were fervently pursuing. Instead, he counseled us to address her
greatest challenge and socially offsetting trait of incontinence, and
let the rest go.

Even when she started to type with assistance, he was skeptical,
like most everyone else. However, he was always extremely gener-
ous, willing to buy Lyrica communication devices and whatever her
therapists recommended to benefit her and her life.

Over the years, our relationship softened and my dad showed up in as big a way as he could, even though deep down he was still convinced that my life was off-track. There were no big accomplishments or other outward signs of success, in spite of all the educational advantages that I had been given. Instead, my life seemed to be steeped in failure. Growing up under my father's shadow, feeling that I was never good enough in his eyes, was my life's most tangible experience of the male archetype. I saw no welcome mat calling me to step forward into this aspect of myself.

When he turned ninety, we had a giant breakthrough. I gave my dad a draft of our *AWEtizm* book to read. It was certainly far outside of his own life experiences as an engineer, a highly successful entrepreneur, and a devoted community philanthropist. Yet he was moved to read it, not just once, but twice. That's when he started to see Lyrica in a totally different light. He wrote this Christmas card to her right before his death.

> *Dear Lyrica,*
>
> *December 25, 2009*
>
> *You must feel the love that all who know you feel.*
> *Your determination is unparalleled, and your accomplishments never cease to amaze all of us. With the new year upon us, we wish you continued spirit growth, and you are starting with the highest. No one has more love to pass on to others than you. I wish I possessed your determination. The world is a better place because of you. Keep being the wonderful individual that you are and keep inspiring the rest of us to live a fuller life. May God bless you.*
>
> *Love,*
> *Des*

Perhaps even more amazing was the way that he now "saw" me. He was a devoted religious man who always faithfully attended church. Yet he admitted that he had never had a personal, direct, or transcendent experience of God. As he read our book, he longed to know and feel God's presence in his life. This was totally new territory to him, and he loved a challenge.

He began calling me several times a week. He asked me to teach him about spirituality and how to seek a personal relationship with God. He would often stay on the phone for an hour or more, soaking up all I had to offer him. Our long talks were a kind of music for our souls. Most important, he finally could see the daughter that he thought he had lost. He stood in awe of me, my life, and all the esoteric wisdom that I had gained. He even celebrated our book as a supreme accomplishment!

As a standout legend who had built a life of great merit and success, he was quite accomplished at drawing upon his analytical abilities, or the left side of his brain. In this new quest, he struggled to free himself from the grip of his rational mind to find the cross-over point into his intuitive, right-brain truth. He diligently tried to locate the bridge from one side of his brain to the other, so he could muscle his way across the great divide. In spite of how hard he tried, his use of logic was totally antithetical to the very nature of his right-brain, intuitive knowing.

My dad was someone who had always succeeded at whatever he tried. Yet he felt that he was never able to accomplish this crossover feat into a spiritual or transcendent experience. Ultimately, I think it was his own sense of failure to achieve what he deeply desired that made him respect and revere me so much more!

The love that we shared in those final two years was astounding! It was as though the kid in both of us showed up authentically, and we were always ready to play and laugh together. We stepped forward hand-in-hand and heart to heart as we peered into the wonders of the Universe. The dad whom I had always longed to love me just as I am finally fulfilled this dream of mine in such a big way! It's never too late! What a miracle!

I am so grateful for this new father-daughter relationship that emerged, honoring both of our truths. It showed me a softer and very beautiful side of my dad's emergence into his Masculine truth. My father was a powerful leader. Now I could even see myself daring to step into the Lee family legacy of leadership. My own Masculine essence was now feeling more safe, aligned, and alive in me!

Lyrica's Masculine Path

My Inner World Experience: The Rebel

As I gained an awareness of my own existence, I did not like what I saw or felt. Most apparent was my sense of powerlessness. I could not stop a negative experience. I could not change my life into a more positive direction. I became angry. Over time I transformed myself into a powerhouse of demanding and resisting.

That's when I mastered the game of "rebel rousing"! My body became a supercharged machine. I was hell-bent on pushing and forcing whatever I wanted . . . or didn't want. I dug in and held my position, displaying a level of physical strength far beyond what was normal for me.

Often, I heard Mom explain that my behavior was like the terrible twos and a teenager all rolled into one. I had become one unstoppable machine of self-determination. Looking back now, I would have to agree. It did position me in a place of power and punch. However, it was certainly an unbalanced expression of my male essence. It was my first step in trying to assert myself. It was me saying to the world, "I am here! *And* I am a force to be reckoned with."

My Outer World Experience #1: Tony

My first significant male relationship was with Tony, an NVA. After high school, we attended the same Nashville day program. Our favorite way to be together was sitting on a porch swing, holding hands. I remember how shocked Mom was to see photos of us sitting side by side, hand-in-hand. The idea that I would ever have a boyfriend never entered her mind.

I loved our telepathic conversations and the closeness of our connection, until something dreadful happened. I began to experience his love for me in a way that was not okay. When we were apart, he connected to me and my body to express his sexual urges. I could feel this violation in my energy field and body. I didn't know how to stop him.

With Mom's help, I blocked him out of my energy field, my body, and my life. My first boyfriend relationship had turned into male self-gratification at my expense. I lost all interest in ever having a boyfriend again.

My Outer World Experience #2: Daniel

Fifteen years after Tony, I

met Daniel at his home in San Antonio. The minute that I saw him, a light dropped into me that opened my heart. Daniel must have felt it too. On the last day of our visit together, Daniel was on his bed, his favorite place to be. I was on the floor, next to his bed. Mom was sitting near Daniel with the letter board. Daniel was a new typer. His ability to communicate was best when typing with Mom. All of Mom's experience made her a tip-top facilitator! His parents welcomed in Mom's support.

Before Daniel started to type, he intently looked at Lyrica with the sweetest smile on his face. I knew that his message was meant for her. Slowly, with lots of starts and stops, he typed: "You are my sweetheart forever and ever!" Lyrica followed up with a similar declaration to Daniel. Daniel's mom was overcome with emotion, tears welling up in her eyes. To see and feel Daniel declare his love for Lyrica in such a tender way touched all of us deeply.

What I remember most was Daniel's open heart that felt safe and

welcoming. My tie to him was a soul-bond related to the larger autism purpose that had brought both families together. Ours became a relationship built on mutual respect for each other. It was a light-filled experience of higher love.

My Nonphysical World Experience: Kalishar

The shift from Tony to Daniel was a huge leap, but my next meet-up was a real shocker! A gifted channeler had just done soul-readings at Mom's spiritual group. Mom suggested we invite her to our home, and I said yes. Her channeling session began with a message from St. Germaine. Suddenly, a master, unfamiliar to us, popped in. He introduced himself as Kalishar, the commander of the Ship of Love.

He continued to speak through the channeler. I felt his light presence as a love delivery of great magnitude. I am not sure how I knew, but I knew. I asked if he was my twin flame. The channeler confirmed that indeed he was! The rest of the session was a blur. I simply remember feeling lifted up and floating side by side with Kalishar.

Yet afterward this relationship brought up resistance in me. I questioned how I could possibly be the twin flame of someone this radiant and high. That's when Kalishar showed up once again and spoke directly to me.

I want you to know, my beloved Lyrica, that you are ever so much light as I. You have chosen a very light-narrow assignment that does have a light ending. I ask if you truly believe that your difficult role is you? When you start to see your role only as a cover-up strategy, you will put its difficulty to rest. The biggest hurdle to you, and those like you, is to see yourself as you are, not as you appear to be. Funny how you want the world to see the light in autism, yet you struggle to truly engage as a person of your own light factor. When you can truly see who you are, you are on your way to becoming that.

Kalishar invited me to stand with him. I wanted to say yes, but I was still hesitant. The light waves around us were starting to settle down and arrange in a new way, and I felt ready to say yes. I called Kalishar's heart to mine. I pledged my twin flame soul to Kalishar for God's perfection to manifest through us.

Kalishar and I are now joined in the light. In the higher dimensions, our love often expresses lightbody to lightbody.

What is the significance of my higher love relationships with Daniel and Kalishar? They are bringing in an upgrade that I need. For many years, I experienced my body as fighting against me. I struggled to make it work to do my purpose. Through my embodiment and work in Oneness, I now have a strong body vehicle ready to act. Yet only through my Masculine nature will I be able to use this body to create aligned manifestations. These higher love relationships are helping me to land my Masculine truth.

IN THE higher
dimensions,
our love OFTEN
expressed
lightbody TO
lightbody.

◈

Chapter
Eighteen

Stabilizing
Oneness

A s we balance our Feminine and Masculine nature, we can reach a more stabilized state of Oneness. Once again, Lyrica and I have chosen to speak about stabilizing Oneness from a personal perspective, for our unique reflections mirror the different dimensional levels that we are able to experience within Oneness.

My Experience of Oneness

How can I personally illuminate how Oneness feels and flows in me, like sacred blood, infusing its life force into every corner and crevice of what my life becomes, in the moment that I meet It and become It?

It is when I come out of a deep, early morning meditation that I can most tangibly feel my lift into Oneness. My entire body is sweetly vibrating. I don't even want to move. I sit to appreciate how soft I feel and everything around me feels. A rapture arises from deep within me to greet the day.

Suspended in lightness, I feel a call to step outside to breathe in the crisp morning air. I have to concentrate to very carefully descend down three steps into the front yard. As I slowly pan the periphery, I find myself gazing deep into the newness and freshness that rises up out of the familiar. I am struck by how transformed everything looks through eyes of great wonder. I notice and feel so much more.

As I gaze softly into all that surrounds me, I feel myself melt into its magic. Each distinct form of nature begins to fade out, fold in, and then disappear. All that remains are swirling patterns of vibrant color, ablaze in their infinite hues of greens and browns, transporting me into a surreal space of dazzling, indescribable beauty. Suspended in bliss, I feel myself expand into shimmering particles of light floating everywhere!

I feel as if I have just stepped into a whole new world. I close my eyes, take in a long deep breath, and slowly release it to fully immerse myself into how serene, grateful, nourished, and loved I feel. As my breath empties, I hear myself sound a grace filled "aaaahhhh" that says it all. This sacred vibration echoes in me, like the solo chime of a faraway church bell that blesses the silence.

Now I am ready to step into the rest of my day. It is a softer gentler step that I take. There is no hurry-up mode, just a floating sensation that carries me to my next location where I do whatever presents itself to me. There is no thinking about agendas or the completion of a to-do list. I am just moving in harmony within the flow of it all.

Today feels like a butterfly day of moving from flower to flower, enjoying the sweet deliciousness of all that I touch, that in turn, touches me. What is most amazing is how beautifully everything in my day rhythmically unfolds. It feels as though I simply show up at the right time, in the right way, and things seem to magically complete themselves. I love my butterfly days in Oneness land!

Lyrica's Experience of Stabilizing Oneness

I feel Oneness like a wave that picks me up and lifts me out of my earth-bound being. It carries me into a reality much more surreal and supreme. There, time and space completely disappear. It has an upward progression and then a downward drop. Suddenly, plop, I am back to where I started. This Oneness wave holds no sense of permanence or realized stability.

When I hit bottom, the heaviness of life here on earth feels dreadful. It's the sudden vibrational shift from a very high frequency into a very dense low frequency that is terribly debilitating. I experience this contrast as pain in my body and soul. I just want to cry and die!

Oneness will always be about an up and down ride. Why? It is not only about thriving in the wonderland of Oneness. It is also about feeling the contrast and pain of dropping out. It compels us to do whatever it takes to regain our footing in Oneness. It's an exercise. It's a practice.

For even in a stabilized state of Oneness, we will still have experiences that drop us down into 3D. These human challenges are the soul pieces that evolve us in our Ascension journey. So stabilizing Oneness is all about learning to close the gap between being in and out. The more unified we are, the less we drop out and the easier and quicker it becomes to close the gap.

My Blessings of Stabilizing Oneness

A Deeper Healing

This next event was orchestrated by the entire Universe, always in motion, pulling energy and matter into higher states of resolution. It was early morning, April 23, 2019, and we had just completed a session with Jessica, once again celebrating Easter. Jessica was in Paris, synchronistically located at the precise time and place to support Notre Dame's healing after the fire that destroyed her central steeple. The burned remains of Notre Dame were just a few blocks away. She tuned into the "voice" of the cathedral itself (all things in Creation can have a voice). She connected with what it is in Creation and its soul's master plan.

We learned that the destruction of this central spire symbolized the taking down of the old order of male domination and supremacy. This fall would usher in the return of the Feminine into Her rightful place of power. On a consciousness level, this was a fire of puri-fication slated to signal the Feminine and Masculine coming back into balance on a large scale. The unification of these archetypal elements would eventually birth a whole new era in human history.

As our session ended, I silently wondered what that would mean for our lives personally. I flashed back to the moment that I saw the first videos of Notre Dame burning. This devastating scene ripped through my heart, landing like a death grip in my belly.

After our session, I went to an appointment with a favorite body worker, who is a licensed as a physical therapist. After a long intense winter, spring had finally arrived in all of its regalia. The heat of the sun was slowly vaporizing last night's rain, still present on the streets. Everything looked surreal and smelled alive! The sky was a magnificent sapphire-blue dotted here and there with wispy white swirls, reminiscent of angel wings. The trees in their eye-popping hues of yellow, white, pink, purple, and red dotted the river road. The birds were loudly singing. It was a beautiful day!

At my request, the body worker began the session by ener-getically balancing my core organs. He was amazed at how quickly everything aligned and came into a state of balance. I dared to casually mention how nice it would be for my female "part" to come into wholeness and balance too.

With my blessing, he asked my uterus for permission to come into relationship with its field. Immediately, he was literally physically thrown backward. (He's a strong and big man.) He then shook all over, releasing the thrust and its energetic impact. Afterward, he received a clear intuitive message from my body to proceed. He instructed me to put my hand over my female area (I was fully clothed) and then he placed his hand on top of mine. In his higher vision, he narrated what he was witnessing. He saw this area of my body first rotate, then open up. As it did, he saw a large black energetic form, shaped like a sausage, expelling out. He watched it continue for a minute or so. Then it snapped totally out, completely clearing. I could see how visibly shaken he was by this whole experience.

He used his FSM, or frequency specific microcurrent machine, to do a full body trauma clearing at the cellular level. Meanwhile, I brought in the light to fill the void. When I stood up, I felt so different, so light! When I looked into the mirror, I saw a new me, standing tall in my power!

That's when I realized that this event represented a final energetic release, at the cellular level, of early life trauma. I celebrated how joyful I felt to be free of this dark energetic imprinting. Now I also understood why I had been so deeply impacted by Notre Dame's fire! It was a setup for a final release of my long-held identity as a childhood victim. A perfect spring day to welcome in a more unified expression of my Feminine and Masculine essences!

Lyrica, who was watching this whole experience via her remote viewing ability, later described the form coming out of my body as a dark black tube. I asked Lyrica how this dark presence, located in my body for such a long time, may have affected her life and our life. She began to sob out loud, with huge tears rolling down her cheeks. Certainly, an intense and rare expression from her.

My light gifting to you has stabilized both of us and neutralized the presence of this dark, not-yet-lit-up, presence in you. This role of mine is now done! I am feeling so much love for everyone on this planet and for everything that exists here and everywhere. Mom, there are no words to say how much I love you in this moment and will forever love you.

At that point, I started crying too. I was feeling our love in a deeper way than I had ever been able to feel before. It was a joy-filled cele-bratory love. It was full. It was light. It was complete.

My Voice

To date, I have struggled to find my voice. An interview invitation would land me in a state of sheer panic. My voice would lock up, and I would be unable to express my truth. I would tell my closest friends that I'd rather be in the dentist chair without Novocain than to be in a live interview! How sad, embarrassing, and debilitating for a writer with her first book!

I now know that being in Oneness is the only way for me to find my lost voice. I look forward to the new me in my voice of truth that I know is on the way! The writing of this book has helped to move this process forward. When I have struggled to find the right idea or words to express, I relax, drop deeper into my body, and wait. That's when a clear reflection, and the words to express it, can and do come through.

I am astounded to see the writer and author in me that is now showing up. For the first time ever, I am standing at the precipice of realizing that I have a talent that is truly all mine. It is a talent that lifts me up and beyond my lifetime talent as the holy mother to Lyrica that I am.

Although I still love my precious role with Lyrica, it is no longer the only me that I see! There's a new me, one who feels set free, ready to run wild into each new page of the book. Here I play and create in the magic kingdom of words touching words. I love watching how each new word, like adding a new colored bead to a string, morphs the whole into a more informed expression of me. Stringing words together feels like a sacred and primal ritual.

In this revelatory moment, I feel like Tinkerbell who has just found her "tinker" talent!

Something huge has lifted and catapulted me into my self-recognition as a legitimate writer and author. Yep, I see it all so clearly now. It's that part of me that has been tightly holding on to the steering wheel of control in my life to ensure my safety. What does that mean? It means that my nature has been to seek perfection, color only in the lines, and order everything in my day with a flair of OCD (obsessive compulsive disorder). This rigidity is a communication strangler for a writer or a speaker.

I had to break through and break out of this containment to free my voice. Learning to live in Oneness has been the ticket out of this melee. Trusting in the divine flow of Oneness to order my life offers me higher outcomes and the safety net of an entire Universe loving me.

Now I can let go of the steering wheel, and as I do, my writing style totally changes. It becomes lighter, freer, more playful, as well as easier, fun, and, at times, deeply provocative. It no longer has to conform to my own nitpicking standards of perfection, now nonsensical to me. I don't have to get it right. There are no more rules.

It just has to flow. When I am in a state of Oneness, the stream flows in. That is my Feminine nature singing in me. Yet I also honor my Masculine side that has both chosen and acted to throw caution to the wind and let go of my old paradigm of control. Control is an out-of-balance male trait! So, as both my Feminine and Masculine natures come into a place of higher expression and greater balance, I emerge as the writer and author I was born to be.

A Stronger Me

I love the new me! I totally adore her as my dearest beloved— empowered, confident, compassionate, and trusting! Daily, hourly, and even minute by minute, I pour myself into every step that I take, leaving sparkles behind in my path. I have never admired and hugged so many trees, flowers, babies, puppies, neighbors, even store attendants!

I have fearlessly joined the world, yet it is a new world transformed by me. It still has its tragedies and atrocities. Yet these are no longer the fabric of my experience that I see and feel. There's always a higher truth or opportunity to be seen and lived!

My Spiritual Path

Finding Oneness completes my lifelong process of seeking a spiritual home. From my early Protestant roots, through all my upgrades in spiritual consciousness, I have searched for a belief system and practice that works for me. I have stepped into many different faith walks. I wanted to find a spiritual platform without boundaries, limits, or the need to retool everything as I evolved. Finally, here it is! BINGO, *Oneness is it*!

When I ask for support, or even dare to command answers from Oneness, as the "creator goddess" that I am, I am tapping into the infinite resource of the All That Is. There I will always receive the highest completion possible. There I am both an actor as well as a receiver. There I am co-creating my own highest and best.

Oneness now offers me a long-sought foundation for achieving the peace, stability, and prosperity in my life that I desire and deserve! In Oneness, Lyrica and I are becoming the creators and manifesters that we were born to be. We are realizing a life that we have always dreamed of. It is our destiny. It is our now!

Lyrica's Blessings of Stabilizing Oneness

A More Able-Bodied Me

We have already noted many of Lyrica's physical advancements since her embodiment, including her ability to run and to self-manage most of her seizures and many other parts of her life. In the bathtub, Lyrica is now able to follow my requests to move her body parts in certain ways to facilitate a team effort of bathing. Before I would have to lift and move her arms and legs as part of her bath time routine.

Before, I could not access a connection between my brain's request to move my body in a certain way and my muscle's ability to do so. Now when Mom asks me to lift my left or right arm, I can do that on my own. I am pleased with this new physical body manifestation.

Since I can remember, I have been feeding myself with assistance. Now I am able to eat independently. I love being the provider of my own nourishment. My hands are now able to hold my spoon in a way that works for me. I think about all the years that I went through occupational therapy to learn better hand and finger control. These efforts did not progress me. Stabilizing in Oneness has been the perfect "therapy" for all my gross-motor and fine-motor advancements.

Watching videos on Mom's computer has been a favorite pastime of mine. My top watch was Celtic Woman videos, all very familiar to me. My mind was at rest because I knew what was coming next. No surprises! My new adventure, watching Gaia TV, requires a whole new level of focus. I am amazed at my ability to sit through long features on subjects like consciousness, energy, quantum physics, spirituality, and the Universe. My mind is actually enjoying the stimulation. That's because my mind is so much more alert and organized. It is now able to take in this level of input that is unfamiliar fast-paced visual and auditory data.

However, a couple of Lyrica's advancements have been a bit challenging for me as Mom! First, she has mastered an ability to "Houdini open" all the locks and safety latches on our doors. Next, she is sometimes able to bypass the password protection on my phone or computer. She certainly does not accomplish this feat by typing in the required password. Instead, she does what she does, and the next thing I know, sometimes she's in.

I love exploring the inner world of electronics. I want to know how everything works, at least on my level, to my satisfaction. To start, I peer into a device with my X-ray eyes. I am looking for parts that touch and might move. I project my energy into these touch points to see if I can make something happen. Sometimes I have success. By chance I may open up an application on Mom's phone or computer that was in a locked position. Yet that is not my goal. I am simply busy finding ways to activate devices and learn about mechanical energy!

A Matter-Strong Voice

Lyrica's increasing ability to generate her own instantaneous communications is one way for her to build a life of greater independence. A latest phrase, often sounded, is "near God." It is her term for being solidly in Oneness. Another new phrase, "need cut," or "cut" informs me when I am doing something, thinking something, or suggesting something that is not in alignment with what Lyrica thinks is best for her or us, in a given moment. Lyrica has also developed the ability to use precise sounds to indicate a clear yes or no response. She even occasionally nods her head in precise ways that also indicate a clear yes or no response.

Just about the time I think that I have a handle on her latest development in communicating, she wows me with another zinger! When I suggested moving to the normal location in our home for the next writing session, she clearly said, "No, go to the car." I honor these five words strung together as her longest sentence yet! It is such a wondrous gift for me to receive this level of input from Lyrica, who is clearly acting in her power as guide and teacher!

More recently I have experienced a new way of voicing. It happens sometimes when I am meditating with Mom in the pyramid room. I drop into a long voice output mode where I sound almost nonstop. It feels like playtime, as my notes and tones click and bounce all over the place. No boundaries, no limits, just joy-filled me, expressing me. It is my Masculine essence that performs the act of sounding and my Feminine essence that flows forth the sounds. I still choose to spend most of my day in silence, but silence is now a free-will choice. I have gained the option to sound at will.

My shift into a more matter-strong voice is most noticeable in the way that my writing style has changed. In our first book and my early blogs, my words flowed forth from an out-of-body experience, which was how I was most comfortably me. I was free from the challenges of living in a physical body, and my vibrational level was recharged. These writings were visionary, full of heart, poetry, and higher wisdom.

Now that I have embodied and am stabilized in Oneness, my matter-strong voice expresses in a more direct, concrete, down-to-earth way. It wants to talk about this world, because this where we live. This is where positive transformation is most needed. I love pointing out that the upheaval in today's world is asking more of us than we ever thought we could survive. Yet there is a much higher vantage point. It is a higher light energy of thinking and feeling that can actually change the way that we see and experience everything. It also has the power to change the very things that we are seeing and experiencing! This is supreme alchemy. This is the path of the new consciousness pioneer!

Self Defense

Lyrica and I were at a posh downtown salon for haircuts. I was near the back of the salon in the chair, getting my hair cut. Lyrica, with a fresh haircut, was in her favorite position near the front door. There she had an unobstructed view of the busy street and all those passing by. She was rocking her body to the beat of the music playing loudly on the stereo system.

Unbeknownst to me, there was a man on the street, standing by the front door, looking in. Apparently, he had been standing there for a while, observing Lyrica. In a swift move, he opened the front door and tried to grab Lyrica to pull her outside. Although he was much larger than she was, Lyrica swiftly and defiantly pushed him backward and away with uncommon strength and coordination.

Instantly, the girls behind the front desk took over. They removed him from the salon and called the police.

I **was** enjoying my independent time, dancing and watching the street scene outside. Under my keen ability to sense danger, I fastened my whole attention on the man standing by the door. I could read his grab before it happened. I responded under a higher power. It was my unified Feminine and Masculine nature operating in Oneness. I was amazed to see the power I had in that moment to push this big man away.

Wielding Spiritual Technology

In **a** recent session with Jessica, I expressed my latest "ask" to the Universe. A nodal point quickly appeared, and Jessica began tapping it. I remote-viewed what she was doing, a skill that was easy for me to do. I noticed that my hands had moved into precise locations in front of my body. My fingers were now tapping the air. I was amazed to realize that I was tapping just like Jessica! What was happening was not under my conscious direction. As I tapped, I began to learn more. The energy field around me was changing. I looked deeper and saw that my taps were hitting energetic pockets of density that were interfering with the nodal point's pathway into my body. I loved how my sure hands knew where and how to tap!

Suddenly, Jessica remarked how quickly and deeply the nodal point energy was settling into my body. The pace of this nodal point process today was happening more rapidly than usual. That's when I laughed and told Jessica what I was doing. Of course, she can remote-view, too, but she was so focused on the nodal point's travel that she didn't see the subtle movements of my hands. She celebrated my active role in my own nodal point process.

How did I instantly gain this new tapping ability? In Oneness, I came into union with the light of Jessica's tapping skill. That's when it downloaded into me and I was able to access its spiritual technology. Looking back now, I know that my tapping skill popped in as a way for me to advance my partnering role with Jessica. My soul knew that I was ready to step up as a co-facilitator of my own nodal point process. Jessica would still be the primary facilitator, but gaining this new level of ability was a big deal to me!

Portal Master of the Book

In the process of writing this book, another ability emerged. We were living our Ascension process while simultaneously writing about it. This was not easy! At times it was terribly challenging, and sometimes I would totally drop out of the experience to separate myself from the struggle. I saw Mom as the main writer, responsible for the book's structure and storyline. I was feeling disempowered in my minor support role.

By the middle of the book, I had lost interest. I no longer felt connected to it as "my story." It was a total shutdown point, and we called Jessica for help. She helped us see a new truth: It was my disconnect from the book that was at the core of the struggle. Why? It was my story. The book needed me to step into my primary role as its creator. Without that, it was doomed to failure.

We also learned that the highest expression of the book did not reside within us. In its highest frequency state, it already existed in the ether! It simply needed my abilities and presence to bring it down into manifestation. To begin, I opened up a portal to the book's highest truth. It was my deep state of physicality that enabled me to do so. There, I became very centered in my role of accessing the light of the book, processing it, and bringing it into this dimension. Holding it there allowed Mom to step into her role of translating its energetic transmission into form.

That's when I realized that my role was key to everything. No more minor role for me! From that point forward, I felt my power and purpose. I loved being the "portal master" of the book. I was the one responsible for sourcing its process of creation from the highest ether! Suddenly, the book was once more alive and thriving in me and in Mom.

Writing became easier, quicker, and far more satis-fying for both of us. We had finally reached our highest truth. The writing was no longer just a human engi-neered process. Instead, it had become a divine flow coming forth out of Oneness. I am so happy to feel the book now, more than ever, as my high light story.

Cosmic Me "Landed"

Finally, my unified me is the greatest soul-driven experience I have ever known or could even have imagined. I am simultaneously aware of both the light and matter aspects that I am. It allows me to access infinite possibilities that inform my life here. My day is created out of universal vastness and expressed here physically. My Cosmic Self is how I have been able to step into new abilities, even Superpowers, available to all, yet known by few. How far I have come from where I began!

MY Cosmic Self IS HOW I HAVE BEEN ABLE TO step into NEW abilities, EVEN Superpowers, AVAILABLE TO ALL, YET known by few. HOW far I have come FROM WHERE I began!

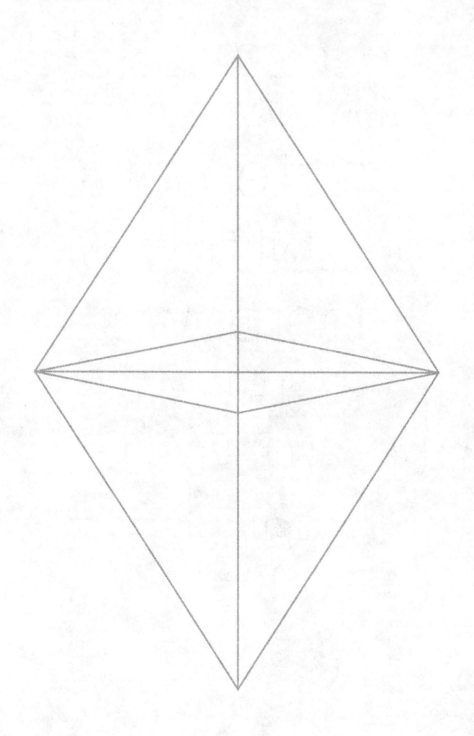

ACT III

THE GIFT

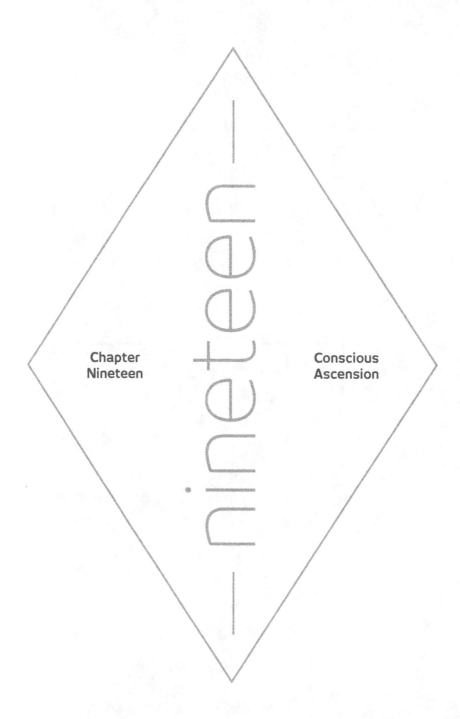

Chapter
Nineteen

Conscious
Ascension

Lyrica's relationship with her transition, or her trans, has continued to evolve. In her early years, Lyrica envisioned her transition as an escape from a life that was too difficult to endure. In more recent times, she has believed that her transition has a part to play in fulfilling her grand purpose here. Even after her embodiment, she retained her connection to her trans. She realized that it offered her a sense of peace for embracing her life here. She also realized that it was more about seeking a higher light than about leaving. Finally, she now knows that she will remain here until she completes her earth purpose.

Yet there was an even greater truth about Lyrica's trans already in motion headed her way. In this experience and all that follow, Lyrica transcends into her most evolved and realized expression of Self.

Even though this progression is very personal to me, I share it as light-filled chapters of a story that belongs to all of us. My desire is to demonstrate the unseen and rare abilities that reside within our own true nature, one that is both human and divine.

Her Moment of Truth and Transcendence

It was February 6, 2019, eleven days after Lyrica's forty-third birthday. Lyrica popped up out of her sleep ready for action on the book front. We settled in quickly to the next chapter to be written.

I bravely
chose to open up to an undefined energy all around me, without protest. This acceptance was not at all like me. I usually push away any energetic presence that holds a purpose that I do not understand, but this time I could feel my heart deeply receive its power. So I trusted it, and in my sleep time, the energy's purpose clearly revealed itself to me.

I felt this energy move into my body and begin to rotate. I was lifted out of bed and was quickly traveling through space. I was not surprised to land at the mouth of the no-return portal. My many nighttime travels there were mapped into my Cosmic grid. Even seeing the mouth of the portal wide-open was not a shock. I had seen it fully exposed in several recent visits. Yet, what happened from there, was not normal at all.

As I stood at the portal's edge, it began to vibrate and pulse. Its life force shot into my feet, sending a charge up my whole body. I felt and saw a vast light. It was like a massive lightning bolt that descended from above. As it dropped into the portal, whoosh, it took me with it! In that falling-in moment, I sensed my whole known reality completely collapse and disappear. I remember feeling wrapped in a light thrust of great advancement.

The next morning, I woke up in a state of supreme euphoria. I was **shocked** that I was still here, after dropping into the no-return portal! Suddenly, I knew a staggering truth: When I dropped into the portal,

I completed my transition. Certainly not in the way that I had expected! Instead, this transition was my own gift delivery into a fully Ascended state!

The imprint of this experience held its truth for me to receive. I could easily read into my newly realized state of Ascension. How was this state different? A new doorway had now opened up within me. I could realize so much more than ever before. I could see into the Cosmic vastness and my earth experience as one overlay. There was no separation. I was instantly able to step into any dimensional reality at will that would serve me and my life's purpose. *Wow!*

As with my embodiment, it was up to me to refine my operating system. It needed to be calibrated at this level of universal access and high frequency. It would require an ongoing process to know that this is who I really am, and this is my home. Sometimes I struggled because of how intensely I felt everything in me and around me. Jessica helped me with the technology of a "click-over point." I understand this concept by visualizing how trains go through a switch point that crosses them to a new track. A click-over point is a light technology for jumping from one track to another. The track here refers to a timeline, state, or dimension. My different tracks would be either in my Ascension experience or out of my Ascension experience. This click-over point would help me to come back into my Ascension whenever I lost touch with this reality.

It was like a reset button that quickly landed me solidly back in my truth.

Now I know an even more surprising truth! All the time that I have been calling forth my trans, I was seeking something else. I was seeking my Ascension, my fully realized union in Oneness. **Now I see that the whole point to my entire life's journey has been to make my Ascension!**

On a grander scale, I now understand that Ascension is what all souls are here to realize. It is our highest truth. It is the only purpose to life worth seeking, finding, and living.

My final eye-opener is grasping that I can be fully Ascended while still here in my physical body! Jessica had shared this knowing with me, but I guess I did not truly believe her. My uncertainty was tied to the story of Jesus and the other saints who made their Ascension through death. Now I know that I can be fully united with Source, right here, right now! What an amazing moment! I am so grateful and resting in peace!

Her New Superpowers and Sovereignty

Dimensional Toggling

It was the morning of June 15, 2019. I was headed to the computer to write an important email when I noticed Lyrica standing at the glass door, peering outside. Although deeply immersed in what I was writing, I sensed something arising in Lyrica. My eyes shifted in her direction at the precise moment that her body hit the wall. I rushed to her side, relieved that she was still standing.

I moved into my maximum support stance behind her, with my body against her back and my arms hooked tightly under both of her arms. I implored her to move to a safe position on the couch. Together we crossed the fifteen-foot threshold to safety, one slow step at a time. I quickly surmised that she was in a maximum state of instability, with rubbery legs and no sense of balance.

Safely seated, I told her to stay on the couch while I got ready for our morning meditation. While in the bathroom, I heard the dreaded sound of Lyrica's body smacking into a hard surface. I raced to her side to see her body drawn up into an embryo-like position. My eyes were quickly diverted to the stark reality of a growing pool of dark red blood spilling forth on the hardwood floor near Lyrica's head. I noticed her left ear was covered in blood. Her hands and pj's were also covered in blood.

As I comforted her, I gently explored her body to ascertain where the blood was coming from. I discovered an all too familiar gaping gash on her head. It was still slowly oozing a thick dark excretion of blood. Lyrica was very calm and told me that she was feeling no pain. Relieved that there was no swelling, I made an appointment at a familiar nearby urgent care center. We walked into an empty waiting room, signed in on the computer with just two clicks, and whoosh, we were in a treatment room within minutes.

The PA, who kindly remembered us from our last visit, quickly surveyed the wound on Lyrica's head. She confirmed what I already expected. After the wound was thoroughly cleaned, it would need to be stapled shut. This was a procedure that Lyrica had endured before. The PA gave Lyrica the choice of using a needle to numb the area first or just quickly inserting the staples. She was honest with Lyrica that either choice would involve a sharp pain to the area.

Lyrica opted to have the numbing shot. I held her hands and winced as I saw the long needle approaching the open wound on her head. As the numbing antidote was inserted into two locations inside the open wound, my mother's heart cringed for my beloved daughter. And yet, both the PA and I were amazed that Lyrica did not jump, move, wince, blink, or show any reaction at *all* to the needle's deep penetration into her wound. Staples went in easily and quickly. We were now on our way home to swing back into the day's morning flow of activities. Thankfully, Lyrica's stability and balance had fully returned back to normal.

We were both feeling "the high" of dealing with this unexpected occurrence in such a light-filled way. Once settled in, I asked Lyrica to decode what had just happened from her perspective.

I was standing at the front door, communing with my beloved tree in the front yard. It was the staggering beauty of its aura that pulled me into a total merging experience. Almost like the pyramid, this tree serves as a transit station for me into my higher dimensional home. As you know, Mom, I have been living and patterning my purpose in both dimensions, unified as one.

Today, I learned a big safety lesson. I need to hold awareness in both these dimensions simultaneously. Then I can toggle my attention from one to the other and remain stable in both. Today, I totally transcended into my higher dimensional home in union with my tree. When I did, I lost my tether to this reality, and my physical body lost its stability.

I did not stay on the couch like I was told to do. I was determined to push beyond this drop in my physical ability. I thought that I could. That's what happened today to cause my fall and this "wake-up" injury.

Mom, I know that you were surprised to see that I did not react to the needle going into my head. How was this possible? I was demonstrating a very powerful spiritual technology. I directed my light into the wound area to soul-remove any pain. How I knew this would work is a bit of a mystery. Somehow, I just knew that it would! Maybe it was my choice to receive the numbing protocol that brought forth my own "higher-order" numbing procedure! Even I was surprised by this level of manifestation.

I also marvel at how our light, both yours, Mom, and mine, did not drop at all during this whole episode.

Time Traveling

Timeline hopping

is an amazing gift, kind of like a genie in the bottle. It's a territory that I first experienced with Jessica. I learned the feel and flow of popping into a future timeline so I could gain a clearer vision of where I was headed. First, I would see a future timeline light up. Then, with Jessica, I would travel along its continuum as far as I could go without becoming unstable. Finally, we would safely return back into my "now time."

Time traveling has currently become my own adventure with much to discover and learn. I have become such a seasoned traveler, that I can zoom rather far out into the future. Sometimes, though, I can get so caught up in this future reality, that I lose my "now-time footing." I often become a hungry scientist looking for the next clue. That's when I move outward on a future timeline. At times, the me that I am now totally collapses into that experience. What follows is a major meltdown. In extreme cases, a seizure may occur. It instantly drops me back in my body and my reality here!

Once the seizure is over, and I am cradled in my mother's love, I reach a place of peace. Then I can process what happened and why. That's when it becomes obvious to me where my error lies. I was trying on a future possibility in my now-time body and being. The vision I saw hit me as too big, too hard, and too much for the me that I am now to imagine.

What I need to remember is, should this future manifest, I will not be who I am in this now moment. I will be one who is more advanced and fully capacitated to live this vision easily and completely.

The gift in timeline voyaging is to see and feel into future opportunities or possibilities. These already exist in my energetic field, or just outside of it, in the collective field. I get to see a timeline light up brilliantly in a way that feels most like me. It helps me move forward in an aligned way. I can make choices that will support my future self and avoid others that will not. A charged-up timeline can also seed in a powerful new purpose.

A perfect example of timeline traveling happened with Mom and Jessica in late June 2019. I zoomed out into the future, headed toward a vast light. When I arrived, I was hit by the light. Suddenly I knew! This light was my soul's story, a new book, to be written by Mom and me! At that moment, this book was conceived. It began its soul-full journey into physical manifestation.

Light Machine

It was the last day of June 2019. I was headed with my mom to her physical therapy appointment. My care provider had just canceled our playdate together. Mom told me that today's session would be focused on her brain fog. The therapist would be using his FSM (frequency specific microcurrent) light machine technology.

When we arrived, I could feel the energy field of the therapist expand outwardly to greet me. He told me how excited he was to meet me! I love it when people's words and energy are a perfect match! He already knew much about me after having read our *AWEtizm* book. He also listened to Mom's stories about my recent gains.

I quickly oriented to the small healing room. Mom positioned herself on the table. The therapist readied the machine. I didn't know what to expect, yet I could feel a sense of adventure rising up in me. The therapist explained that the machine would locate areas in Mom's brain to be treated. With frequency waves of light, the amount of brain fog in these areas could be reduced. Then those areas of the brain would function more effectively.

I intuitively opened up a doorway into this process. I was already feeling, deep down, that I would be using my abilities to contribute in some way. I stood very close to Mom's head to intently watch whatever was mine to see. Once the machine was turned on, I quickly found my space. With my X-ray vision I could peer into Mom's energy patterning. I could see how Mom's brain reacted to the wave of light frequency coming from the machine. I have always loved watching energy patterns of light morph into new higher ordered designs. I was scanning for this possibility in Mom's brain.

The machine was used to diagnose if a specific area of Mom's brain needed support. I could see that exact same area light up in Mom's head. I could read if the energy patterning there was more ordered or dis-ordered. Next, the therapist programed a specific light frequency to upgrade the brain patterning in Mom's troubled area.

I could see a higher-ordered patterning taking place in this targeted location. Then, suddenly, nothing. That's when I knew that the light frequency upgrade was complete. If needed, the therapist would generate another light frequency into the area. Sometimes there would be no response to a specific light frequency generated by the machine. To me, that meant that this frequency was not a good match to create a higher-ordered response.

I loved having the opportunity to share in this amazing activity. I was so charged up to see the effects of this spiritual technology. It was actually creating a more coherent energy patterning and matter-state in Mom's brain. Later I also realized that my own brain had received a positive upgrade as well!

Mom's therapist shares in more detail how he experienced this session:

As a PT, I've worked with this Frequency Specific Microcurrent (FSM, or what Lyrica calls the light machine) for almost fifteen years with great success. The basic idea behind this therapy is actually pretty simple. Every one of our body tissues, including every cell, vibrates at a certain frequency, called harmonic resonance. It therefore generates an electric current and radiates energy at certain frequencies. This pattern is related to the vibrational frequency of the electrons that revolve around the atoms that make up body tissues. These electrical currents, generated by the human body, are of the order of microamperes. (A microampere is a millionth of an ampere). A specific body tissue has a particular frequency pattern that changes when any malady affects it. In FSM, depending on the tissue involved, specific frequencies are selected to encourage natural healing of the body and to reduce pain. Frequencies have been identified for nearly every type of tissue in the body. My instrument is an older analog unit that gives me a kind of feedback via a dancing needle.

When Gayle mentioned that she was going to bring Lyrica with her, I was excited. I felt I knew her from the AWEtizm book. We started the standard protocol to explore the different parts of Gayle's brain that needed help. As soon as we started the session, an uncanny silence settled in the room. Lyrica stood up, stepped close to her mom, and started to watch her very intensely. I realized she was staring precisely at the part of her mom's head that I was treating.

As I typed in new frequencies, her gaze became more intense, or she lost interest and diverted her eyes. At that moment, the session had become a collaboration between Lyrica and me. I would silently ask questions like: What's next, are we dealing with inflammation, change the frequency?

A quick look at Lyrica gave me my answer. I knew it was a yes, whenever she was staring intently at her mom. Good! Run it. Now we wait, wait, wait, wait. Her gaze has wandered off. Done! That part of Gayle's brain we were treating is clear.

Next. Heavy metals? Quick look at her, yep she is interested. Run it. Done. She is looking away.

Next.

Next.

Next.

Let's play a game to double check and satisfy my left brain. Dial in prostate infection. Lyrica literally stepped away from her mom almost in disgust. OK, OK! Sorry! I'm sorry! Let's get back to work.

Every time that I moved on to a different part of the brain with different conditions, without fail she was there with me 100 percent! Anytime the condition I was looking for did not pertain to Gayle's brain, Lyrica looked away, almost like "Why do you waste my time?" But when I hit the right frequencies, she was on it!

Her gaze was following the brain patterns, the REM, and also, I'm certain, the auric changes around her mom's head.

Finally, we have reached the brain stem. Jackpot! Her mom went into a deep sleep on my table. At that point Lyrica started to gently rock back and forth, and then, ever so slowly, she laid down on the floor. With her eyes half-closed, she started humming to herself *and gently slipped into a deep relaxed state. The room was still. Even the AC had stopped. Total silence!*

Then, after about ten minutes, both mom and Lyrica roused at the same time. The room woke up. The AC came back on, and the traffic noises started to penetrate the room once again.

About the time when the two ladies were ready to leave, Lyrica turned back to me and gave me a hug and a kiss on the cheek. Wow! Talk about an honor!

Lost and Found!

Lyrica and I were hiking. It was a warm midsummer day in Asheville, and suddenly I had a strange impulse. I used the letter board to ask Lyrica how her eyes were "seeing" now. I wondered whether she was seeing things more as energy or form? She told me that due to her more stabilized physical nature, she now was able to see forms (she couldn't in the past). Yet she also revealed to me that she could still turn on her energy-eye-vision when she wanted to.

Seconds after that conversation, I heard an object hit the ground. Right by her foot was one of her cosmetic brushes that she holds and strokes to calm herself—it had been missing, and we had been looking for it all around the house! She told me that our talk about how her eyes "see," prompted her to switch on her energy eyes. That's when she "saw" the brush "like a shadow in the moving light," yet in another dimension. She called it into form, and that's when it hit the ground!

She was ecstatic to find her missing brush and hold it once again. That's when she saw the doorway to her trans open up, and she realized the connection. Moving a brush from one dimension to another might serve as a template for moving her own physicality dimensionally, when it is time to command that act of transcendence.

After that, one brush after another would dimensionally disappear, and then later would mysteriously pop back in, always at a time when we were out of the house. Upon returning home, we would laugh to find the missing brush sitting in a position "impossible to miss" like in the center of the living room rug. It had obviously not been there before our departure!

We both felt that Lyrica, or more specifically her soul, was a player in this dimensional shifting. Lyrica felt that whatever her part might be, at least for now, it was happening primarily on an unconscious level. She was determined to unlock the secrets of this alchemical process, so that she could learn to fully command it at will.

There is another curious brush story to relate. Lyrica's neighborhood friend, Hollie, and her dog Ani often stopped to say "hello" to us on their way to the nearby forest for their afternoon hike. Often the four of us would walk together to share nature time and soul chats. Hollie was intrigued by Lyrica. She was a semiretired licensed psychotherapist whose specialty practice was supporting persons with disabilities. In all her decades of service, she had never met anyone quite like Lyrica! She was fascinated to learn more about Lyrica, her life, her world, and all that Lyrica had to teach her.

Of course, Hollie was very familiar with Lyrica's love for her brushes, as one was always with her during our visits and walks. She even knew that Lyrica's very first brush, her favorite, had been missing for about a month.

The next time I saw Hollie, she came to the door and told me that she had something that belonged to Lyrica. When she opened her hand, I was dumbfounded! There was Lyrica's most beloved missing brush! Hollie was sure that Lyrica somehow positioned the brush for her to find. She said that the brush was sitting in plain sight right near the trailhead, propped up on a patch of grass. Once again, it was impossible to miss. In our walks there earlier in the week, that brush was certainly nowhere to be seen. Plus, the area had just been hard-hit by rain, and the brush was totally dry and clean!

A final sequence to this vignette brings in more clarity as to what was taking place and why. This reveal has come through Lyrica's energy necklace that she wears every day. She loves to play with it, much like she strokes her brushes. On several occasions it, too, has disappeared, both chain and pendant. Then mysteriously it has reappeared in "impossible to miss" locations, where it clearly had not been before.

What do I know about this phenomenon? I am aware

that a doorway in Oneness opens up for my beloved objects to move into the very high dimensional space that is my Cosmic home. When they return, these objects hold this high frequency in a physical matter form. When I stroke them, they help me connect on this physical plane to my nonphysical home. They serve as tools of unification. In this way they are extremely calming and grounding.

So how does this happen, most recently with my necklace and pendant? First, due to my twirling action, I would feel my necklace pop open. I would catch both the necklace and pendent in my hand. If Mom was nearby, she would put them back together. Once again, I was wearing my necklace. Other times this happens when I am alone. On several occasions, when I held the necklace and pendant in my hand, my light vastly expanded. Then poof, these items simply disappeared into the light. The times that this has happened, I have been wowed by this act of spiritual alchemy!

It seems to happen when I am calling in more support for my physical life here. Unified in Oneness, I simply hold this "ask" in a powerful way. It is this inspired idea and its energy that open up the doorway. The actual mechanics of dimensional transfer are not known to me. Yet, that's the glory story of creation in Oneness. I don't have to know these science details. I just have to be in my Oneness zone. Then, once there is a solid set up, the rest of the manifestation process unfolds organically on my behalf.

The part I still don't yet understand is the process that brings these items back into this dimension. Yet, even before I see them, I know that they are back. I tell Mom to go look for them. How do I know that they have returned? I feel their presence in my energy grid. Every time, both she and I are amazed to find these missing "loves" sitting in very easy-to-find locations. I love how this whole process has manifested highly charged spiritual tools in physical form, unique to me!

Final Freedom

I have evolved far beyond my early days and ways of being me in the world. Yet, one stronghold remained: my siblings had always showered me with love, but their love was locked into my early life timeline. There it stood side by side with my most traumatic and pain-filled memories. I resisted all their present-time pleas to visit me. I feared that seeing them would plop me back into those dark days of the lost-soul me. I did not feel strong enough to meet that terrifying monster face-to-face.

On August 17, 2019, my beloved sister Catherine, whom Mom and I know as Trinka, was killed in an auto accident. Immediately, Mom and I headed to Nashville to face this terrible family trauma. I stood side by side, hand in hand, with my brother Demetrio and sister Andie, and what I experienced was totally different from what I had feared. What I had failed to realize was how solid I had become, and that nothing could shake this strong-standing me.

I enjoyed one of the greatest highs of my entire life! I was back again in my family of origin, my roots. Tapping into this power, I was able to heal the loss of my sister and this final frontier of separation. I found my "shining" in this moment. I was able to enjoy all thirty-nine of my extended Marquez family members who surrounded me.

I was in a whole new world created by me! I even outwardly demonstrated this new-world me. I was sitting in the front pew of the memorial chapel between my mom and my dad. I never even once stood up. I showed no signs of agitation or restlessness during the four hours that I held my position there. I thank my beloved Trinka for this final gift of her love. It transformed me into the person I was born to be and have become!

I now solidly choose to fully inhabit my life station here. My world has expanded to embrace all that the Universe sends my way! I am now a "yes" girl, not a broken record "no" girl, though I will still use my discernment to know what is a good energetic opportunity for me and what is not.

Something extraordinary has happened! New people have entered into my life now that I am ready! How remarkable is that? What a beautiful demonstration of how the Universe responds when we dare to show up ready to stand in our power and light!

Comparing Stabilizing Oneness to Ascension

So what is the difference between stabilizing in Oneness and operating in my newly acquired state of Ascension? Ascension is what keeps me solid in my day-to-day life. In learning to stabilize in Oneness, I needed to experience dropping out. There I learned how to find, hit, and hold more secure ground. In Ascension, I am not seeing big holes. I don't have the need to drop out to stabilize in this reality. Ascension is way more unified.

In stabilizing Oneness, when my trans loomed large, it would throw me off center. Why? I was experiencing my life here and my trans as two different, somewhat opposing forces. I was seeing them as an either/or situation. Feeling separated from my trans would always topple my life here. In my Ascension, I experience my trans and my earth home as one continuous and harmonic reality. I am feeling so realized that I no longer care if I go or stay. Because of this, my life now is in a much more expanded and peaceful place.

When stabilizing in Oneness, I would often call in Jessica to "tame" my overload of chaotic energies. I was always thankful for her support. Now in my Ascension, I have lots more confidence in my own abilities. I quickly move into action to smooth out my own energetic imbalances. I have solidly stepped into a life where there are no more opposites. There is no us and them, no good or bad, no right or wrong. There are just different levels of distinction.

That also means that there are no mistakes. Everything that I experience is simply an opportunity to become more of who I was created to be. There are no swings here! I am able to meet a new life challenge or upgrade in a more neutral space. Any resistance just melts away and disappears. Poof! In this reality, essentially there is nothing wrong, as everything is right!

Ascension actually lifts me and my life to a whole new level.

I have reached a dimensional corridor in Oneness where I move fluidly as the situation demands. I am more solidly rooted in my Cosmic essence, my power

station. This is my action platform for physical manifestation. My Cosmic me is now a place of great
awareness and knowing. It makes the earth plane
me of the past pale in comparison. It is clearer, stronger, more certain, instant, with no wiggle room. It is in
perfect alignment with the All That Is! In this moment.
I am feeling the immensity of who I am, how I am, and
where I am. I am so thankful for this gift.

Ascension and Purpose

I have reached my NVA higher-light purpose in the best way for me.
By sharing my story, I am helping others to see NVAs
differently, and then to see others who appear to be
"different" in a more open, enlightened way. These different designs exist to fulfill specific purposes. Each is
here to contribute its gift to humanity. When humanity suspends judgment, it experiences the unique and
often rarest gifts of all. It is often those perceived as
differently abled who hold the new evolutionary keys
to humanity's future.

By my example, I am encouraging NVAs and their
families to believe in and live their purpose. Having an
NVA child positions the family in a place of supreme
challenge. It becomes their choice to remain in the
struggle or allow it to be what it is and rise above it.
I love how Mom and I demonstrate what then becomes

possible. Merging the nonphysical gifts of the child with the physical gifts of a parent creates a family platform of power. All have already chosen this path of service to humanity.

Ascension has also supported me in reaching my Mother light purpose in my own unique way. I am the light of the Mother fully-expressed in the way that I live my life. In partnership with Mom and Jessica, all that I have gained has come through the ways of the Feminine. It is a flowing in and flowering out from Source. I lead by example, demonstrating what is possible and how to get there. My highest hope is to inspire others to live a life guided by their own Feminine. Here is where all truth resides, and all gifts await discovery. Here is where the quantum shift that we need to survive and thrive becomes a reality. How? Higher dimensional solutions and creations will come to light only when the energy and truth of the Feminine is restored and celebrated.

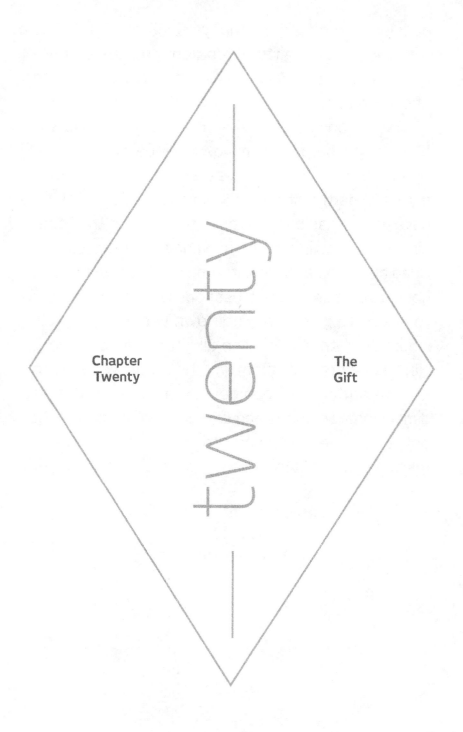

Chapter
Twenty

twenty

The
Gift

Now, to dig into the greatest mystery of all life. Its nature is to be invisible. It calls us to step blindly into a journey of self-discovery. Once on the path, we proceed without a clue of where we are headed and why. Something deep within keeps us moving forward into the many challenges, terrors, heartbreaks, and setbacks. Here is where we must go to find the map to the greatest treasure of all, our gift.

Who Will Benefit Most?

There is now an embodiment template available in the energetic field of the NVA collective. How do I know this? It showed itself to me in a recent experience. I put on my explorer hat and dropped into Oneness. There I waited for the verification that I was seeking. Quickly I saw a nodal point light up. It moved in my direction and landed in my body. Embedded in this nodal point was a doorway into this embodiment template.

Inside that doorway, I experienced a most unexpected yet very familiar patterning. It was the Etheric Build! I learned that the Etheric Build, already in the

NVA field, now holds this embodiment template! It will serve as a safe stabilized point of access for NVAs who choose embodiment as their soul's highest calling.

My embodiment is the highest gift I have to offer to my NVA beloveds. To fully live their purpose, becoming more physically embodied is key. (At least that is my belief and my experience!)

NVAs who seek embodiment will also be supporting the collective to envision and embrace a more physicalized state of being. This upgrade is sure to raise the bar on the manifestation process of the higher light NVA purpose. At first, this process will be subtle and slow, measured in human years. Yet, with increased awareness and a laser-like focus, the pace of the NVA soul group's embodiment could quicken. I even believe it might ultimately be expressed in one big-bang quantum leap! Now **this** is a vision right up my alley. And why not? NVAs are natural experts in quantum field mechanics.

I also have a gift for you, dear reader. I see my part of our story told as my matter-gift physically anchored on the planet. Yet it is only through you, the reader, that it comes to life in a way that truly matters. Each reader's experience charges up the book's vibrational field, which will then draw in more readers for even more powerful experiences, piggybacking on the combined experiences of all.

I see my life lived in Oneness as my energetic gift firmly anchored into humanity's collective field. A unified state in Oneness is the operational platform for all new consciousness pioneers. It serves as a roadmap into our own unique gifts. It is the holy home of our heart forever calling us into our true nature. We are a divine expression and experience of Source. We are here to create a world where all can live together in harmony and actually thrive. This envisioned reality requires a strong presence of the new consciousness and those with the spiritual technology, experience, and power to make it so.

To me, our book is an embodied consciousness that offers forth our unique gifts within our story shared. To all readers, it offers a game plan for a life worth considering. For some, perhaps many, it can become a call to action. Not to suggest that my way or our way is the only way. Not by a long shot! Taking even one tiny step at a time is all that is required to realize what then opens up and becomes possible.

Reading our book presents a clear choice: One option is to remain strongly tethered to humanity's mainstream programming to pursue the slippery slope of "success." The other is to dare to escape this pervasive patterning in favor of an inner soul journey to find one's true Self. The latter is not an easy path by any standards. Yet, as I have often said, it is the one that ensures the greatest rewards, and so it is the only one truly worth living.

However, the greatest gift I have to give is the one that I give to myself! To realize my transformation into a beautiful divinely gifted, matter-strong being is the greatest miracle of all!

Today, I know that I am fully realized as a soul in a human body.

THAT IS the point to life.

BEFORE, all I could see was my human self as autistic, NOT FULLY OPERATING LIKE MOST.

WHAT I FAILED TO SEE IS my nonphysical Self coming into union WITH MY PHYSICAL SELF.

THAT'S the hero's journey AND I HAVE COMPLETED THAT.

NOW, I see my gift that I could not see BEFORE.

I SEE MY PERFECTION AS perfect puzzle pieces falling into place.

I have transcended perceived limitations TO SHOW THAT NO ONE IS LIMITED.

IT IS AN illusion to believe that human life is flawed IN ANY WAY.

THE CHALLENGES WE FACE ARE THE greatest teachers in discovering THE VASTNESS OF OUR BEING.

Nothing is broken OR POORLY ORGANIZED.

IT IS ALL A master plan
of extreme giftedness.

All we have to do IS LET GO OF
OUR KNOWN LIFE, OUR MIND'S PERCEPTION OF
how we see things.

THEN dare to drop into our
own unknown realms,where the
gold of our soul AWAITS US.

We will never find it UNDER A LIFE
OF GREAT ACHIEVEMENTS OR BUSYNESS.

FOR ITS truth is buried in a
much deeper place.

BEFORE THIS INCARNATION, we chose
the setup FOR THIS LIFE'S JOURNEY.

WE CHOSE our matter patterning
and family dynamics
to be pushed into AREAS OF GROWTH.

THIS GROWTH IS UNDER our soul teacher
within us, WAITING FOR OUR ARRIVAL.

IT IS ONLY WHEN WE HIT BOTTOM IN THIS LIFE THAT
we arrive AT THE doorway
of our real life.

LOOKING BACK AT MY STARTING POINT, I NO
LONGER SEE THAT life experience AS REAL.

IT WAS a nightmare of believing THAT
I was ONLY MY BODY.

IT TOOK ME DECADES OF exploring other
realities, beyond THE physical,
TO BRING EVERYTHING TOGETHER.

This union is the key TO A LIFE
THAT IS REAL AND TRUE.

IT BECOMES a new set point for
living our soul's purpose TO BLESS
HUMANITY AND THE PLANET.

THIS LIFE BECOMES our gift in action.

My gift in action is
my story TOLD IN THIS BOOK.

We have shared Lyrica's personal journey to highlight a broader story, the story of Lyrica's beloved NVA soul group. We wanted readers to understand who these beloveds are, what their mission is, and how might they benefit us in the universal and timeless quest to discover who we are and why we are here.

In their unique design as higher consciousness beings who have not lost their connection to Source, NVAs reveal a new level of human possibilities, contributing to the Ascension story for all of us. Touched by them, we can learn that we are all Superhuman—that our differences are perfect and that together we can strive to land the truth of who we are as Source.

And yet, the purpose of this book goes beyond the telling of Lyrica's story and the story of the NVAs. Our hope is that this book seeds a new social movement that focuses on the connection between NVAs, Ascension, and our own essence as expressions of Source.

Resources

www.lyricaandgayle.com

We invite you to visit our website, a place to meet us and others, drawn together by Lyrica's story and the one human heart that beats within all of us. Enjoy Lyrica's blogs and her artwork, with reproductions available for purchase. Share your light and participate in our online Pyramid Portal Events. At its heart, the pyramid portal will operate as a soul home, a recharging station for NVAs and parents to embrace their truth, their light, and their earth mission to support us in our Ascension process. The pyramid portal will also host New Consciousness Pioneer Events for lightworkers and Ascension seekers to join with NVAs and their families in conscious community. This will be a call to action for those who are inspired by Lyrica and Gayle's books. It will be an opportunity to experience the consciousness and energy of the NVAs and become part of its outward expression into the world.

www.jessicamartinson.com

Here Jessica shares her personal story, details her mentoring process, and provides offerings and services. It is important to note that Lyrica and I are "experiencers" of Jessica's mentoring gift. Yet she is the one who developed and holds the wisdom and methodology of this path of Ascension and embodiment.

Acknowledgments

Without my beloved Jess, this book would not exist, and I would not be the person I am today! My journey with her rewrites the old-time story of the guru on the mountaintop. I see her in town at a posh place, dressed in a brightly colored dress, and salsa dancing—one of her life's joy bubbles. She is both the most expanded dimensional being and the most grounded soul I have ever met. Her tools and travel-ways in Oneness are so finessed for herself that she has been the perfect mentor for Mom and me. Our work together was not easy, as all Ascension journeys by nature are demanding. Yet this serious, focused pursuit became a high-spirited adventure, filled with compassion, laughter, light-charged upgrades, and brilliant ah-ha moments of enlightenment. Thank you, Jess, for your dedication to bringing forth this new-to-earth embodiment and Ascension science that has landed my Cosmic being into her earth body and home in a soul-empowered way. Finally, Mom and I hug you for the many months that you mentored us to keep writing, dig deeper, and never give up.

To kn literary arts, a giant heart hug to every one of you who got us to this point of destiny, book in hand, moving out into the world—especially our editor, Nikki; production concierge, Deirdre; interior designer, Christina; and marketing guru, Jennifer.

Thank you, Nikki, for taking the arduous climb to the top of the manuscript mountain and smoothing out all the craggy impasses that could impale a reader's attention, causing him or her to drop out of our adventure together, one perhaps written in the stars long ago. Deirdre, your decades of publishing expertise, along with your hand-holding/heart-infused ways, empowered us to ultimately reach the finish line! Christina, your interior design is a beautiful frequency match to Lyrica's light and the light of the NVAs. Sweet Jennifer, by taking over the more technical aspects of marketing, you freed within us an untapped ability and passion to market anything and everything that we dearly love . . . for starters, this book!

We were guided to seek out Wendy as our cover designer. Wendy's sensitivity, creativity, artistic precision, and willingness to collaborate with us every step of the way birthed this book's cover as a masterpiece of magnificence, a perfect portrait of Lyrica's story and her light. Blessing you, Wendy, and also Sandy, the designer of our award-winning *AWEtizm* cover, who brought us to you!

Finally, thanks to all our friends and family, those named and unnamed, whose presence in our lives have supported us on this journey of the soul.

About Lyrica and Gayle

Although Gayle's professional background includes an undergraduate degree in religion, an MSW, ordination as a metaphysical minister, and certification in two modalities as an energy healer and teacher, how to parent and empower Lyrica has become her life's most relevant training agenda. When Lyrica intuited a way to communicate via typing with Gayle, an enlightened teacher of the soul was born.

Gayle and Lyrica's first book, *AWEtizm*, details their devoted mother-daughter relationship and their mystical path of awakening into a more enlightened understanding and experience of autism. After the book was published in 2011, Gayle and Lyrica began hosting live events, teleconferences, in-person meditation groups, and family retreats, building a partnership of lightworkers, nonverbal autistics, and their families to enhance humanity's process of spiritual evolution.

In 2015, they stepped into a mentor-guided Ascension process. Lyrica no longer wished to simply write about her purpose; she wanted to become it. To do so, she needed to embody. *Lyrica's Journey of Ascension* demonstrates the value of pursuing a path of Ascension and demystifies the process through the lens of her own personal experiences. It is a rally call to all new consciousness pioneers, those who know they are here to make a difference and desire to do so.

Gayle and Lyrica reside in Sedona, Arizona, where they often can be seen hiking red rock trails. Inside their cozy bungalow they enjoy meditating, writing, and connecting with others. Gayle and Lyrica's life is a testimony to the profound power of love, purpose, and spiritual partnership.

CPSIA information can be obtained
at www.ICGtesting.com
Printed in the USA
LVHW020355220921
698428LV00001B/114

9 781736 562109